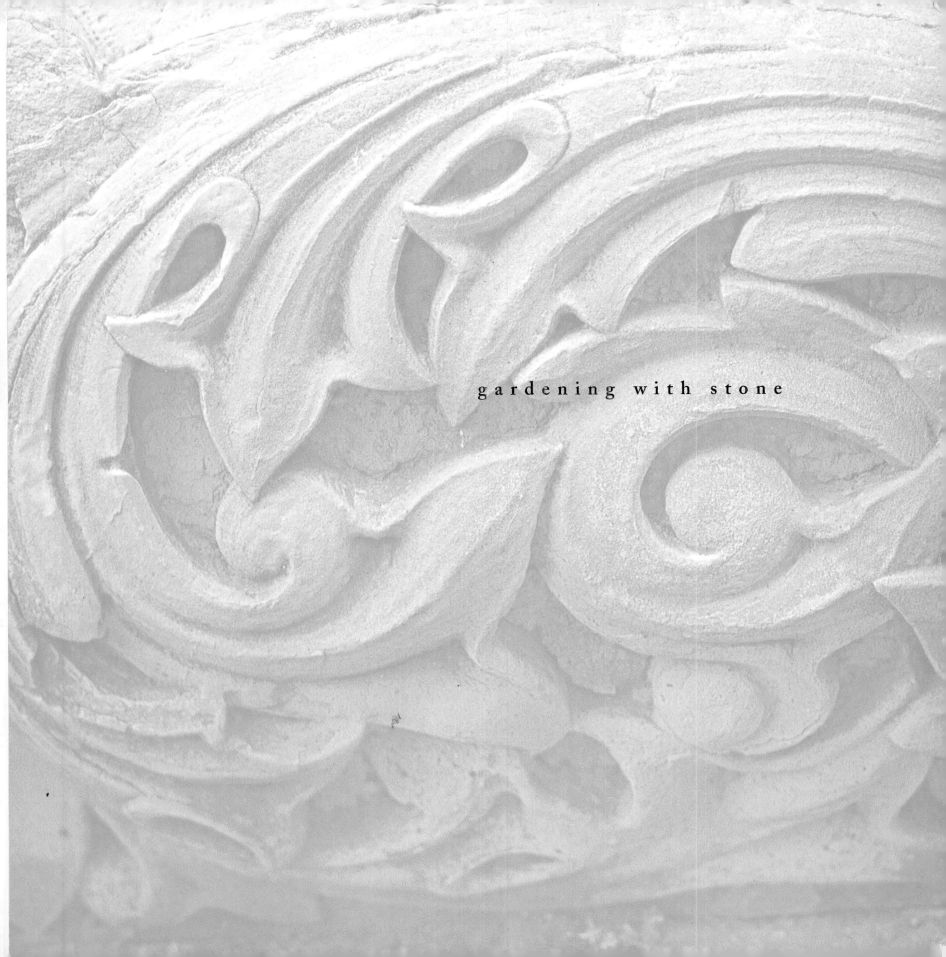

gardening with stone

GARDENING WITH STONE

Using Stone Features to Add Mystery, Magic,
and Meaning to Your Garden

Jan Kowalczewski Whitner

photographs by Linda Quartman Younker

Macmillan · USA

MACMILLAN
A Pearson Education Macmillan Company
1633 Broadway
New York, NY 10019

MACMILLAN is a registered trademark of Macmillan, Inc.

Cataloging-in-Publication Data available
from the Library of Congress.
ISBN: 0-02-862134-4

Manufactured in China.

10 9 8 7 6 5 4 3 2 1

Designed by Amy Trombat

*Additional Photo Credits: Allan Mandell, page 41; Phil Wood,
page 76; and Steve Whitner, pages 13, 130, 133, 142, 158, 160.*

contents

acknowledgments

First of all, thanks go to Linda Quartman Younker, my co-worker and friend, whose photographs express what words cannot.

This book also was made possible by the following individuals, who gave generously of their knowledge and time: In the South, R. J. Dykes III of New Orleans, Louise Wrinkle of Birmingham; Holly Blount, Kenneth Treister, Suzette Kores, and Ian Ball in Miami; Janet Alford in Vero Beach, Florida; Ryan Gainey in Atlanta; and James Morton in Savannah. In the Southwest, George Pingitore and Suzette Lucas of Scottsdale, Michael Zimber in Santa Fe, Bill Hays in Albuquerque, and John Troy of San Antonio. In the Denver area, George Bates, Marcia Tatroe, Panayoti Kelaidis, Susan Yetter, Mike McLaughlin, and Sandy Snyder. For access to Midwest gardens, I am indebted to Hal Martin, Ruby Smith Love, and Wendy Perks Fisher. In the Northeast, to Laura Palmer, John Kelly, and Penelope Maynard in the Hudson River Valley; Jonathon Keep in New Jersey; and Harriet Sornberger in Connecticut. And on the West Coast, Tina Peterson, Hendrikus Schraven, Tom Berger, Nora Scully, Rosina McIvor, Florence Walker, Phil Wood, and Art Wolfe of Seattle; Rex Zumwalt in Tacoma; Mike Shur of Wenatchee; John Platt and Allan Mandell of Portland; the staff at Tor House Foundation in Carmel; Tom and Erna Morris of Monterey; and Peter Newton of the Napa Valley.

Thanks also go to my agent, Elizabeth Wales; and at Macmillan, Barbara Berger, editor; Amy Trombat, designer; and Sharon Lee, production editor.

And, as always, heartfelt thanks to SW and the furry boys, who make home the greatest place to be.

. . . they live among us but they do not know us,

and we do not know them. But sometimes

they speak to us . . . .

Octavio Paz

Plants, water, and stone: These are the natural design elements from which all beautiful gardens grow. Garden writers have examined the landscaping uses of plants and water in exhaustive detail, but the third element—stone—still awaits the attention it deserves.

Stone is eloquent, and it speaks in many voices. To philosophers, it speaks of time, endurance, and the inevitability of change. To poets, stone speaks both deeply and directly about the bone connection between humans and the physical world in which they live. To scientists, it speaks of the earth's composition and development, and of the history of ancient life forms buried deep within its stony layers. And to artists, it speaks of myriad textures, colors, and forms waiting for the human imagination to give them shape and meaning.

For gardeners, stone is an infinitely suggestive material, because they can draw on all of these associations when they add it to the landscape. Some of our most imaginative gardeners have used stone to transform ordinary plots of land into the cumulatively rich and evocative landscapes we all hope to create.

Gardening with Stone: Using Stone Features to Add Mystery, Magic, and Meaning to Your Garden surveys how stone has been used as a fundamental design element in a broad array of American gardens—historic and new, classic and innovative, stately and whimsical, public and private, and designed by professionals or completely "homemade." Our focus is on those magical, metaphorical stone features that will spark the imagination, as well as on creative design solutions to common landscaping problems.

garden
styles

Asian Gardens The Bones of the Garden

According to Chinese folklore, a troll-like demigod named P'an Ku spent twenty thousand years sculpting the universe from an enormous mass of primary granite. After carving the sun, stars, and planets with a mallet and chisel, he sacrificed his body to form our own world. Mountains sprouted from his skull, rivers coursed from his veins, and his teeth and bones became magical rock specimens and minerals hidden deep below the surface of the earth. According to this legend, rock is the universal primordial substance, and a stonemason, P'an Ku, was the architect of the world.

The Chinese—and their neighbors the Japanese, who also see spiritual and magical properties in stone—believe that a garden should represent the most essential features of the earth. For this reason, they consider stone to be the most important element that can be included in the design and construction of all gardens. Although they may lack water and even plants, Chinese and Japanese gardens always possess stone, usually in groupings of rocks, specimen boulders, gravel, and cobblestones; more rarely, cut stone appears in building blocks and flagstone. Although both cultures share a fundamental reverence for stone as a primordial element in the garden, they each use it to create very different kinds of design effects.

China possesses a vast and varied topography, including mountains, steppes, deserts, valleys, and forests that range from temperate to jungle-like. Of all these various potential models, the Chinese have chosen the mountain landscape as the major inspiration for their gardens. This choice is based on deeply layered cultural, spiritual, and artistic traditions in Chinese society, which regard mountains as the homes of gods and powerful natural forces (such as thunder and rain) and as the natural habitats for sages, philosophers, and poets to wander through in quest of knowledge and enlightenment. Similarly, Chinese painters have always used jagged mountains and steep, forested ravines as subjects for their artistic explorations of line, shape, texture, and the play of light and shadow on objects. Chinese gardeners are attracted to deeply eroded limestone and sandstone with fantastical shapes and pocked surfaces—they believe spiritual power is concentrated in the rocks' whorls, holes, and striations. Both individual monoliths and the "mountain formations" in Chinese gardens surge with an extroverted energy, even exuberance, that stands in contrast to the calm monumentality that stones typically possess in Japanese gardens.

(Dr. Sun Yat-Sen Classical Chinese Garden, Vancouver, British Columbia)

The charged, highly compressed energy of the "false mountains" seems about to explode in this Chinese courtyard garden, giving it a kind of drama that no other landscaping style approaches. The paradox lies here: Even though this pile of rocks sits surrounded by whitewashed walls and pebble-and-mortar flooring, viewers can easily abandon themselves to the illusion that an entire mountain stands before them, losing any sense of scale and proportion by immersing themselves in details of precipices, outcrops, bluffs, and grottoes. Thus, as sculptor Richard Rosenblum notes, Chinese gardeners use finite objects, especially stones, to evoke an infinitely deep landscape—the entire world. (Dr. Sun Yat-Sen Classical Chinese Garden, Vancouver, British Columbia)

The most precious specimen rocks in Chinese gardens come from the waters of Lake T'ai near Suzhou, an ancient city famous for its intricately elegant courtyard gardens. The silty waters of the lake carve the soft limestone into fantastic shapes that Chinese gardeners value for their abstract beauty of line, texture, and color as well as for the spiritual energy they are thought to possess. And because the Chinese believe that a t'ai hu rock has both an "interior landscape" and a relationship to the space outside it, placing these specimen stones so that they look and feel "right" in a setting is one of the most demanding design challenges a Chinese gardener faces. Here, a t'ai hu rock is positioned so that the shadowy interplay of its interior hollows and knobs is dramatically apparent, while at the same time its relationship with other rocks and plants, as well as the flat white wall and the lacy moon gate behind it, is also fully explored. (Dr. Sun Yat-Sen Classical Chinese Garden, Vancouver, British Columbia)

The Japanese design tradition quietly stresses natural-looking groupings of stone, with densely textured rocks; cherts, gneiss, and various granites are especially prized. Although these mostly metamorphic rocks originally were formed in extreme conditions—during periods of dramatic change in temperature, stress, and pressure deep below the earth's surface—the Japanese gardener values a weathered rock, with smooth, rounded edges and a patina of age. Perhaps this love of aged, "settled-looking" stones is natural among a people that lives on a relatively young chain of mountain islands featuring active volcanoes. In a suggestive contrast, sedimentary stones, which were formed during long eons of erosion, are valued in Chinese gardens for their sharp edges and highly grooved surfaces—characteristics usually associated with geologically young stones.

(No matter what its geological age, a stone that has remained buried and has not been exposed to the processes of erosion will look younger than a stone —of any geological age—that has been on the earth's surface and exposed to the elements.)

Japanese garden style has a measurable influence on American gardens today, whether it is imported wholesale or adapted to our various topographies and palettes of plants. The relative abundance of Japanese gardens open to the public has played a role in expanding the style's popularity. In recent years, several authentic Chinese gardens have opened to the public in North America—is it simply a matter of time before this rich and ancient tradition begins to influence American home gardeners? (See the Appendices for a list of Chinese and Japanese gardens that are open to the public.)

Because urban Chinese gardens always sit in courtyards surrounded by walls, they usually have dramatic, centrally positioned features that will focus the visitor's attention inward, toward the garden's heart. Ponds rimmed by stones often play this crucial role, providing a rich and compelling sensory experience through the interplay between rock and water, sun and shadows, and ripples and a mirror-still surface. This garden was built in 1938 on the grounds of the Four Arts Society in Palm Beach, Florida, in the style of a courtyard garden typical of Hangzhou, a port city on China's eastern coast where many water gardens are found. Hangzhou and south Florida possess similar climates and an abundance of limestone for making gardens; so the Four Arts pond with its taro stands, water lilies, and island stepping-stones made from local limestone charmingly and authentically replicates the look of its Hangzhou counterparts. (Chinese Courtyard, Four Arts Garden, Palm Beach, Florida)

Mabel Choate, owner of Naumkeag—a luxurious country estate in the Berkshire Hills of western Massachusetts—traveled to China in 1935 and spent a month in Beijing visiting gardens and buying Chinese statuary, garden furniture, and carvings. Returning home, she asked landscape architect Fletcher Steele to create a courtyard garden on her estate that would incorporate authentic Chinese design principles and also accommodate her recently acquired collection of garden art objects. The garden, built between 1937 and 1939, features an austere pavilion with an inclined stone panel set into the steps, which lead up to its main terrace. The dragon panel was originally sited in the old Imperial Summer Palace outside Beijing, where only the emperor, carried in a litter, was allowed to traverse it; all other courtiers and functionaries had to step around the elaborately carved stone slab, so thickly encrusted is it with symbols of imperial grandeur and power. (Naumkeag, Stockbridge, Massachusetts)

Steele believed his most difficult task in designing the Chinese courtyard garden at
Naumkeag was making it seem authentic while also looking "at home on a New England
hillside." To establish the correct atmosphere, he used Chinese building materials, such as
the pavilion's blue roof tiles made in a factory dating to the thirteenth century, stone rail-
ings imported from an old garden in Suzhou, and marble planter boxes lining the stone
path that leads to the pavilion. His solution to making the garden feel right in an
American country setting came only after the interior garden was already built. Relying
on drawings and photographs he had accumulated during his own visit to China in
1934, Steele designed an encircling wall reminiscent of ones he had seen in Beijing's
Forbidden City. This wall focused the Chinese garden inward, while providing a long
curving boundary between it and the rest of the estate. The brick-and-stone construction
appears perfectly at home with the surrounding Massachusetts countryside; and the moon
gate, added as an afterthought in 1955, prepares visitors for the exotic garden within
The wall's marriage of brick and stone is successful because Steele allowed the wild energy
of the stone to burst through the formal geometry of the brick with a dramatic effect.
(Naumkeag, Stockbridge, Massachusetts)

In 1986, nature photographer Art Wolfe visited the sacred mountain of Hua Shan, which rises in jagged peaks above an enormous plain in China's central Shensi province. Wolfe was inspired by the mountain's landscape, which he described as "granite spires among twisted pines." He wanted to evoke its spirit in his Seattle garden, which coincidentally rises from a level surface at one end to a steep slope at the other, echoing Hua Shan's geographical setting on a miniature scale. Wolfe began by placing two 12-ton granite boulders gathered from the foothills of the nearby Cascade Mountains at the bottom of the slope; then he carved a pond and stream out of the side of the slope with a backhoe.

Additional stone monoliths were placed around the pond and stream to replicate mountainside vignettes, which can be enjoyed at close range as one walks the twisting path that climbs to the top of the slope. Wolfe planted full-size Japanese maples (Acer japonicum *and* A. palmatum) *and ponderosa and Japanese black pines* (Pinus thunbergiana) *among the granite spires and then softened the entire composition with mosses he collected at clearcuts. The mosses brought in seeds and roots of other Northwest native groundcovers and woodland plants, including various ferns, salal* (Gaultheria shallon) *and oxalis* (Oxalis oregana)*, which add a distinctive Northwest touch to the garden, bringing it into full visual harmony with the surrounding regional landscape. (Art Wolfe garden, Seattle, Washington)*

When Frank Lloyd Wright established a school of architecture, Taliesen West, outside Scottsdale, Arizona, in the 1920s, he and a small band of dedicated students constructed the campus's buildings, terraces, and walls from a mix of sedimentary and igneous stones that they gathered on site. The concrete and rubble structures at Taliesen West echo, to some extent, the architectural style of Teotihaucán, Monte Alban, and other historic sites built centuries earlier in the high central valleys of Mexico—the massive shapes and dramatic lines of Taliesen West's structures complement the surrounding mountainous, dry landscape in the same way that the Mexican sites echo theirs. Wright added panels of Chinese porcelain figures to some of the walls, including this one standing opposite his office off the school's main square. Despite a complete disjunction of materials, colors, textures, and cultural allusion between the wall and the panel, Wright's collage works artistically—perhaps only genius can imagine and reconcile such unlikely combinations successfully. (Taliesen West, Scottsdale, Arizona)

Japanese gardeners often achieve complex hardscape
designs by exploring the visual relationships among
stones of a variety of sizes, colors, textures, and
forms. Here, stone features range in size from gravel
to cobbles, edging stones, and a small horizontal
boulder; in color they come in all the grades between
cream, light gray and charcoal; and in form, from
sharp gravels and the sculpted outlines of the formal
lantern to the soft, natural line of the small boulder.
The interplay of patterns created by these different
qualities is rich but not frantic—perhaps the vignette
retains such a serene air because the plants surrounding the stone features have been carefully selected to
bind them all together by means of a quietly harmo-
nious background. (Portland Japanese Garden,
Portland, Oregon)

In contrast to the eruptive force of rock piles typical in a Chinese garden, the boulders in a Japanese garden usually settle into the landscape with a serene inevitability. Each boulder is placed so that its individual character shines through, but the relationship between all the rocks in the composition also is given its full due. Stone features are often used in Japanese gardens to establish and manipulate scale and proportion. Landscape painter Ikune Sawada, for instance, used several monumental boulders (granite specimens from Washington's Cascades Mountains) as the focal point in his eastern Washington garden. The boulders create a sweeping, spacious scene, although the garden's actual dimensions are quite compact. (Ikune Sawada garden, eastern Washington State)

Stone is the material of choice for most pathways in Japanese gardens. This is for practical reasons: Stone is generally easy to acquire and inexpensive; a well-laid stone path lasts forever; and stone pathways do a good job of keeping feet dry and protected as visitors walk through the garden. But there are other reasons why stone is a favorite path material. Because it acts as the foundation of the larger landscape, stone seems the metaphorically right material for visitors to tread upon. Stepping-stones can be staggered to slow the visitor's pace down, so that a selected scene can be enjoyed at leisure; in this sense, carefully structured paths actually help shape the visitor's experience of the garden. And most important from an aesthetic point of view, stone materials can be combined to create interesting patterns in the pathway itself.

Landscape architect Hoichi Kurisu designed this path so that small, roughly shaped granite stepping-stones, which are mortared together for a slightly formal effect, alternate with larger, darker, wilder stones as the path goes across a stream. The flat stepping rock at the lower left is large enough to permit visitors a comfortable viewing space as they travel either way on the path. If they are traveling left to right, then the stone lets them slow down to enjoy the stream before they cross it; if they are traveling right to left, the stone signals that they are moving from one area of garden (shady woodland) to another (a more formal and open area with gravel flooring raked in patterns). The small grindstone (center) adds another layer of pattern and texture to the pathway scene. It is the buildup of such well-designed details that makes a garden scene seem visually rich and exciting. (Anderson Gardens, Rockford, Illinois)

There is comparatively little use of formal stone features in Japanese gardens, but this area in the Anderson Gardens represents two of the most popular forms that such features can take: stone pavements and sand gardens. The "sand" used in this garden is actually a decomposed granite, which retains the shapes into which it is raked for more than a week, if the area where the garden is laid out is sheltered from the wind. (American gardeners report that chicken grit, sold in seed and feed stores, substitutes well for decomposed granite.) The informal wave patterns raked in the sand play off the formality of the gravel material itself—strictly geometric patterns, such as crisscrossed squares or complete circles would make the feature seem entirely formal in overall effect. The straight-edged and mortared stone pavement that cuts through the sand garden also feels formal, even though the individual pieces of stone used in the pavement have irregular edges, which are echoed by the forms of the stone steps in the upper left. Such natural touches help tie this formal area into the rest of the garden, which features the asymmetric informality typical of Japanese gardens in general. (Anderson Gardens, Rockford, Illinois)

Perhaps the most crucial challenge in designing an informal pond is to make the meeting points between the water and the stones that edge it seem completely, inevitably natural. Arranging the stone edging in too regular and symmetrical a pattern results in an unimaginatively predictable effect; and simply tumbling boulders around the pond's rim in a hodgepodge makes them look—in the words of English rock gardener Reginald Farrer—like a "devil's lapful" of stone.

Ikune Sawada used an arrangement of granite boulders with broad, horizontal lines to create a restful but powerful design for the edge of his pond. Some of the stones overhang the water, and the mirror images they create on the water's surface help tie the stone and water together visually. On the upper left, Sawada has almost submerged an entire boulder in the water, which not only suggests that the stones above and below the waterline are parts of the same geological formation but also gives the pond a feeling of great depth. Groundcovers around the bottom edges of the boulders soften the transition points between stone and water, while linking the aquatic plants to the land vegetation nearby. Sawada created these details to emphasize the natural points of connection between stone and water and, by extension, between the pond and the landscape surrounding it. (Ikune Sawada garden, eastern Washington State)

In Japanese gardens, stone lanterns often combine aesthetic and practical functions, such as casting a moody light on a pond at night while marking a bend in the path that surrounds the pond, so that visitors won't lose their way in the dark. Many stone lanterns are rather formal in style and typically have sharply cut features; but Allan Lobb, a sculptor and collector of Japanese folk art, built this wild lantern from stones he collected on site in his naturalistic Japanese garden, which is located on sloping forest land in western Washington. Lobb stacked the roughly shaped stones like a small abstract sculpture; a more formal lantern would have seemed out of place in such an informal garden, but this lantern's pleasing rusticity complements the surrounding landscape's mood. (Allan Lobb garden, Preston, Washington)

Formal Gardens Stone Geometry

The sixteenth-century Mughal ruler Babur, who conquered much of present-day Afghanistan and northern India during a reign that lasted more than thirty-five years, was a noted patron of the arts, especially the art of garden making. He created ten major gardens in his capital city of Kabul alone, adopting the classic Persian garden style of symmetrically paired planting beds bordering straight-edged water channels and rectangular reflecting pools. In a book of memoirs known to history as the *Babur-nama*, Babur kept notes of how his gardens were constructed, including detailed lists of the flowering plants and fruit trees planted in them. One entry describes how he made a garden out of a pleasant stopover site in the hills above a village just northeast of Kabul: "Under great plane trees, green, shady, and beautiful . . . a one-mill stream flows constantly; formerly its course was zigzag and irregular; but I had it made straight and orderly, so the place became very beautiful."

That last comment sums up the most basic tenet of the formal gardening tradition as it evolved in the ancient Middle East, spreading to Rome (and from there to the entire European continent) and to the Islamic world (which eventually encompassed Asia Minor, central Asia, and northern India): Order is beauty, and by imposing order on the natural landscape it becomes transformed into something that is more nearly perfect and, therefore, more beautiful—a garden. This love of order and symmetry is apparent in some of the earliest garden plans extant in the Western tradition. Egyptian tomb wall paintings dating from 1400 B.C. show neat rows of date palms and fig trees lined up around geometrically shaped pools and enclosed rectangular atriums with paired columns leading to the adjoining rooms of the roofed main dwelling. The tradition still held strong three thousand years later, when in the early seventeenth century Shah Jahan began the Taj Mahal and its gardens at Agra in northern India and, more than a continent away, André Lenôtre designed Versailles for Louis XIII outside Paris. Some of the dominant design features at the Taj Mahal and Versailles are remarkably similar, such as the flat, hierarchically structured beds of parterres laid out before the massive, symmetrically designed palaces.

(Swan House, Atlanta, Georgia)

The world's great formal gardens depend on perspective, symmetry, and organized geometric shapes to achieve their impact; and cut and trimmed stone was the predominant building material used to construct the walls, terraces, water channels, and promenades characteristic of this garden style. Many of the historic garden estates in the United States, built from colonial times through the early twentieth century, adopted the classical or formal style, although they were built in an age when brick, stucco, and poured concrete often replaced stone as the building material of choice. But there are enough formal stone features in such public gardens—including Dumbarton Oaks in Washington, D.C; Swan House in Atlanta; Filoli in Woodside, California; and Vizcaya in Miami—to provide plenty of inspiration to home gardeners. The strict geometry and axial perspectives that characterize formal garden design may look their most imposing in these kinds of large gardens, but the use of designs that stress balance and symmetry and of building materials with crisp, hard edges will introduce formal touches to even the most intimately scaled private garden.

The gardens at Atlanta's Swan House were designed in 1928 by architect Philip Trammell Shutze, who took the hill gardens of sixteenth-century northern Italy as his source of inspiration. In the best spirit of European formalism, he used axial views, large promenades, and symmetrically balanced accent features with classical motifs, such as these columns and stone urns flanked by parterres and topiary. (In the midst of these features, does the rampant eagle symbolize a vigorous nod of acknowledgment to the garden's American setting?) Elsewhere on the grounds, precipitous flights of steps and a massive water cascade sculpted in series of shells descending a steep bank also evoke the Italian Renaissance gardens, whose grand stone features were typically used to establish an architectural framework for hilly garden areas. (Swan House, Atlanta, Georgia)

A Florida garden plays with classical allusions, its gleaming Grecian columns lightening a dark corner underneath a banyan tree. The massive rubble wall behind the arbor sets off the garden's dramatic tropical foliage. (Ian M. Ball garden, Coconut Grove, Florida)

This atmospheric sunken garden began its existence as the stone foundation of a building that housed the second oldest African-American church in the state of Illinois. The church stood adjacent to a limestone quarry that supplied the building stones for most of the public and private buildings in Galena, an old port town on the banks of the Mississippi River that possesses many fine examples of nineteenth- and early-twentieth-century domestic architecture.

The church burned down to its foundation and remained abandoned for many years, until its present owner, the artist Hal Martin, bought the property in the 1970s. Rather than bulldoze the remaining foundation or simply cover it with fill and soil, Martin decided to exploit its ornamental possibilities by making it into a formal sunken garden. He built a raised pool in the garden's center to act as its focal point and allowed ivy and ornamental vines to smother the surrounding stone walls. There is a melancholy but pleasing air, reminiscent of a Roman ruin, in this garden that is underscored by the pinecone finial that stands at the top of the stairs leading down toward the pool—stone replicas of pinecones were used to mark off the boundaries of country gardens and estates in classical Roman times. (Linmar Gardens, Galena, Illinois)

This courtyard garden is floored with elegant Italian marble squares that, along with thick borders of ferns and other plants with tropical-looking foliage, evoke the look of a Victorian conservatory. The marble squares were laid down in 1882, at the same time the adjacent house was built, to create a cool and light-reflecting passageway through a shady corridor, which runs between the back garden and the street. The plant border and its collection of early nineteenth-century marble statues—which perfectly complement the marble floor's ornate formality in tone, color, and texture— were added by the present owners in 1992. (Lion's Head Inn, Savannah, Georgia)

In the mid-1980s, James Morton decided to add a new room to his small garden in the historic district of Savannah. The original garden featured two formal compartments composed of rectangular planting beds, so he decided to vary the pattern by making the new area a circular planting bed, which he filled with numerous Ilex vomitoria, a small, shiny leafed holly that makes an excellent subject for topiary. Morton kept the rounded ilex so tidily clipped and shaped that one day a neighbor, Louisa Farrand Wood, herself a formidable gardener and the niece of landscape architect Beatrix Farrand, told him, "I'm so tired of seeing these green donuts—please, do something interesting with them!" Morton decided to turn his clipped hollies into the sixteen points of the compass and placed an armillary in their center as a focal point. Recently, he added the circular path of large flags of Tennessee shale, placing them over a shallow bed of sand and gravel and leaving enough space between the slabs to plant small arrangements of ornamental herbs. This arrangement demonstrates how a thoroughly successful classical look can be achieved in even a small garden space, using a minimum of stone features that are supported by formal plant palettes. (James Morton garden, Savannah, Georgia)

New Orleans's historic Vieux Carré was founded in 1717 by French settlers, and it retains many architectural legacies of its early French (and later, Spanish) inhabitants. For example, many of the district's historic homes are built around interior courtyards, which feature large slabs of stone as flooring. The stone slabs are prized for tidily withstanding the torrential downpours of rain characteristic of New Orleans weather. If sluiced with water, the stone flooring also serves as a cooling medium during sultry summer afternoons, as the water slowly evaporates from its damp surfaces.

New Orleans sits on a vast fluvial plain through which the Mississippi River winds its way toward the Gulf of Mexico. The plain itself is underlain by thick layers of unconsolidated sediments, so there is little local stone available for construction. Before the 1840s, most trading ships were powered by wind and sail, and the port of New Orleans was visited by sailing ships from Europe and the eastern U.S. seaboard, all of which carried stone as ballast. These seemingly inexhaustible supplies of stone from the quarries and fields of New England, France, Scotland, and Spain were used to build New Orleans's houses, courtyards, and streets between the early eighteenth and the middle nineteenth centuries. The water runnel crossing the left side of this stone flooring is a traditional French architectural detail, confirming that the courtyard was built before 1794, when an enormous fire that engulfed the French Quarter demolished most wooden constructions but left many stone features intact. The strikingly architectural forms of palms and other tropical plants look especially dramatic against the courtyard's severe stone floors. (Soniat House Courtyard, New Orleans, Louisiana)

Formal Spanish gardens often feature flagstone courtyards with central fountains. The fountains play a major role in establishing such a garden's ambience: Their trickling waters both cool the hot summer afternoon air and provide tranquil background music when people gather to enjoy the balmy night breezes. A fountain courtyard in the west Texas town of Fredericksburg shows an interesting mix of Spanish design (a tradition belonging to the early Hispanic inhabitants of this part of Texas), local stone materials, and traditional wall-building techniques brought in by German immigrants, who began settling in Fredericksburg during the 1840s.

German stonemasons quarried local limestone and shaped it into blocks. The blocks were then mortared together to build the enclosing courtyard walls. (Most of the older homes in Fredericksburg are constructed from the same limestone blocks—their fresh, creamy colors and textures add a crisp charm to the town's simply designed and constructed cottage homes.) The courtyard's flooring is made of limestone crazy paving from the same source, and the base of the Spanish-style fountain contains mortared river cobbles that were taken from one of the countless streambeds that twist through the nearby west Texas hill country. (Nimitz Homeplace Courtyard, Fredericksburg, Texas)

From the late nineteenth century on, garden
walls in many south Florida communities
have been built from quarried blocks of
limestone and coral, which are the locally
available stone materials of choice. The
rough-hewn grandeur of these walls is often
quite striking—this one evokes associations
with the heroic ruins at Mycenae and
Tiryns, strongholds of Homer's Bronze Age
Greeks. The wall's ancient Mediterranean
ambience is underscored by the presence of a
classical torso, which is nestled in a niche in
the weather-eroded stone blocks. (Ian M.
Ball garden, Coconut Grove, Florida)

In Christian symbolism, the rose is
an embodiment of the tender
sweetness of Mary, the mother of
God, and the well represents the
inexhaustible depths of divine
wisdom. This garden in
California's Napa Valley presents
both symbols in a formal setting of
straight-edged planting beds
backed by pruned-and-shaped rose
standards. The medieval marble
well is Byzantine and features,
incised along the rim, a mysterious
script that baffles scholars, who are
unable to identify its origins.
(Newton Vineyards, St. Helena,
California)

Fletcher Steele used an otherwise nondescript slope of lawn at Naumkeag as the setting for this inspired rose garden. Designed to be viewed from above, the pink gravel ribbons loop together eleven floribunda shrubs in a playful pattern that reads as half swag, half parterre. The novelty of this garden plan resides in treating a nongeometric, nonlinear pattern as a formal design—the rhythmic regularity of the gravel path's curves and the uniform background provided by the lawn combine to create the qualities of symmetry and repetition, which a formal design requires. (Naumkeag, Stockbridge, Massachusetts)

These hard-edged pavers set into lawn add a classically elegant touch to a small southern garden. Made of a pink Arizona flagstone and set in sand, the pavers save wear and tear on a well-traveled patch of grass and keep visitors' feet dry when the area is muddy or wet. (Private garden, New Orleans, Louisiana)

Natural Gardens Stone and the Romantic Realists

From their beginnings, Chinese and Japanese gardening styles were firmly rooted in naturalistic designs, organic forms, and informal planting schemes; but it took European gardeners until the eighteenth century to shake off the strictures of formal design and look to the natural landscape for inspiration. Why the dislike among earlier Western gardeners for using mountains, forests, and natural ponds as sources of inspiration? Perhaps it is because medieval and Renaissance gardens in Europe were meant to serve as allegorical representations of Heaven or Paradise, and so they were designed in the spirit of ordered perfection that the concept had always conveyed in the Western tradition. Since nature is rarely if ever ordered, balanced, and symmetrical, it could hardly provide inspiration for the creation of a perfect garden. (In contrast, of course, Chinese and Japanese gardens are meant to evoke the essence of the natural world; and for that reason, formal features and planting styles have seldom played an influential role in their designs.)

But during the Romantic era that swept Europe during the late eighteenth and early nineteenth centuries, traditional philosophical, political, and artistic movements were abandoned, to be supplanted by a revolutionary new taste for the natural and the free. Now artists and philosophers deemed nature's irregular and unforced beauty superior to the "artifice" of perfection that earlier generations had valued; it was during the Romantic era that garden designers developed a corresponding appreciation of the natural landscape and its features.

Romantics had a special affection for mountains, stony cataracts, and picturesque ravines with boulders tumbling down their slopes, because they believed these kinds of dramatic scenes represented nature at its most inspiringly sublime. The stone features in the wild sections of some famous European gardens of the eighteenth and nineteenth centuries, such as the naturalistic cliffs in Paris's Bois de Boulogne and the astounding cascade and Neptune basin at Germany's Wilhelmshohe, testify to the power of this inspiration.

(Private garden, Bow-Edison, Washington.)

In the United States, the painters of the Hudson River Valley School showed a fervent appreciation of the Romantic qualities of the natural landscape as early as the 1820s. Thomas Cole and Frederick Church painted lush and luminous landscapes of upper New York State and New England and, in turn, inspired a later generation of painters (including Albert Bierstadt and Thomas Moran) to portray the more spectacularly rugged landscapes of the American West. Mountains, cliffs, canyons, and buttes were often the focus of these painters' works—they valued massive stone formations as the chief jewels among the continent's natural treasures and as the most dramatically artistic symbols of the country's moral and spiritual aspirations.

The grandeur of America's landscapes also inspired the work of prominent American garden designers during the second half of the nineteenth century and well into the twentieth century, beginning with the titanic figure of landscape architect Frederick Law Olmsted (1822-1903), the designer of New York's Central Park, where his use of curving, sweeping lines, natural boulder outcrops, and native vegetation was revolutionary in its time. It continued with his son, Frederick Jr., and nephew, John Charles, whose landscape architecture firm, Olmsted Brothers, designed park systems, planned communities, and private gardens throughout the United States into the 1950s. Two midwestern designers, Jens Jensen (1860-1951) and O. C. Simonds (1857-1931),

followed the same basic tenets as the Olmsteds throughout their influential careers: to maintain the essential qualities of the natural landscape, while opening up its dramatic and ornamental possibilities; to incorporate natural views into the landscape plan whenever feasible; to preserve pleasing natural contours and features in the garden itself; and to use a preponderance of native plants. Because all of these designers planned park systems for numerous cities and communities, many of which still remain relatively intact, and because they were all pioneer educators in the evolving profession of landscape architecture, their influence remains strong today among contemporary landscape architects and garden designers.

If America's great urban park systems often feature naturalistic designs, not many of its historic estate gardens (most of which were private in origin) are wild—perhaps there seemed to be too many spectacular natural sites outside their gates to compete with! Virginia's Gunston Hall, North Carolina's Biltmore Estate, Florida's Vizcaya, and California's San Simeon—to name just a few—take their inspiration from formal European styles, rather than from the natural surrounding landscapes. But there are some notable exceptions. New York State's Innisfree and Manitoga, and Washington State's Ohme Gardens, for instance, use boulders and cliffs—to quite stunning effect—as the major garden features in their naturalistic garden designs.

Garden designer Penelope Maynard's elegant woodland garden sits amid the
rocky slopes and ledges flanking Mount Aspetong in New York State's
Westchester County. Using the landscape's natural contours, as well as the
granite found on site, Maynard designed an informal architectural framework—granite outcrops and low mortared retaining walls built of the same
stone—with the purpose of establishing a series of level resting terraces in an
otherwise steeply graded hillside. Following Maynard's design, master stonemason Vincent Bueti curved the retaining walls to echo not only the lines of the
nearby granite outcrops but also the natural contours of the slopes on which they
are sited. (John and Penelope Maynard garden, Bedford, New York)

natural gardens

This courtyard contains the kinds of juxtapositions between formal and informal design elements—such as straight-edged concrete pavers playing off of rough basalt columns—that add an interesting visual complexity to even the smallest of garden spaces. Because this scene lies just outside large windows in the living quarters, evergreens (including rhododendrons, hellebores, azaleas, and ferns) were planted to provide year-round viewing interest and to soften the visual impact of so many stone features arranged in a relatively confined area. This garden, designed by landscape architect Randall Allworth, convincingly conveys a sense of stone's natural power and grandeur, even when it is sited in a formal courtyard setting. (Private garden, Seattle, Washington)

The bone-deep complementarity of textures, shapes, and lines featured in this natural garden is the design element that gives the scene such remarkable drama and strength. The rough-hewn wall stones and the sinuous curves of the low stones flanking the gate, which echo those of the enormous granite boulder behind it, and even the shaggy bark of the conifers and twisting madrona all celebrate natural forms and surfaces with a complete, focused intensity. (Dennis Duban and Kevin Montgomery garden, Fidalgo Island, Washington)

Granite boulders and a floor of small rounded pebbles provide an elegantly spare backdrop to a group of woodland plants in a Northwest natural garden. The interplay of colors and textures between the stones and the surrounding plants makes a satisfying composition: The boulders' warm undertones echo the adjoining plum foliage and deep pink blooms, while their sharply angled edges are complemented by the hard leaf margins of the salal (Gaultheria shallon). *(Private garden, Bainbridge Island, Washington)*

Garden designer Susan Yetter wanted her small urban lot to resemble the naturally dramatic landscape of the high plains that push into the eastern flanks of the Rockies near Denver. She used a regional red-and-buff sandstone to construct the ledges, drifts, and screes characteristic of these arid plains and mulched the garden floor with gravel to conserve moisture and suppress weeds. Yetter, who wanted the plant palette she introduced into the garden to represent some of the diversity of the plants naturally found in the plains environment, designed the space for year-round interest: The species crocuses, tulips, and early flowering alpines of spring are supplanted by summer's perennials (including natives, water-wise hybrids, and cultivars that resemble natives). In the fall, a seasonal tide of grasses rolls over the garden; and in winter, the sculptural qualities of the rock formations are most apparent, especially when they are lightly covered in snow. (Susan and Robin Yetter garden, Denver, Colorado)

A stone bench, made of the same basalt as the cliff behind it, underscores the Stonehengian grandeur of this garden scene. (Ohme Gardens, Wenatchee, Washington)

Hal Martin's Illinois garden is sited in a long-abandoned limestone quarry; here he has used some of the mined-out quarry walls as a naturalistic backdrop to an installed waterfall. Martin turns a potential visual liability— the gouged and scarred remnants of a mining operation—into a dramatic feature that heals the landscape while acknowledging its recent history. (Linmar Gardens, Galena, Illinois)

Historic dry-laid stone walls, constructed from fieldstone that was gathered and stacked by farmers who cleared the fields for crops two centuries ago, line the routes of many old roads in New York State and New England. This wall is built with a flat, flaky shale used in combination with rounded stones, which local gardeners identify as a type of quartz. (Millbrook, New York)

Placing formal ornaments in otherwise completely natural settings can be a most effective design technique; here a sculpted angel contributes a classical grace note to a west Texas meadow filled with spring wildflowers (Private garden, Fredericksburg, Texas)

Water-Wise Gardens Chiaroscuro in a Dry Landscape

Perhaps the twentieth century's greatest contribution to the development of garden style is the "ecological" garden. There have been naturalistic garden styles before—the landscapes created by Capability Brown in the mid-eighteenth century come immediately to mind—but there is a fundamental difference between the naturalistic and the ecological garden. In the former, the appearance of naturalness sometimes comes at the expense of much artifice. Brown, for instance, often demolished hills and filled in valleys to achieve the seamless sweeps of meadow and slope that were his signature look. But in the truly natural garden—the ecological garden—the surrounding topographical and climatic conditions will govern the overall design, as well as the choice of the plant palette and hardscape materials. As a result, such a garden often looks and grows like a refined version of the natural landscape surrounding it.

In many regions of the United States, particularly the arid West, water is a precious resource; and environmentally sensitive gardeners try to limit their use of it by growing water-wise and native plants, often set among natural-looking hardscapes made from local materials. For this reason, many water-wise gardens offer particularly rich examples of local stone used in informal hardscapes that echo regional design styles and motifs.

Water-wise gardening also often takes place in areas of the country where the sun and its patterns of light and shadow play a dramatic role in how the garden looks, and no designer will want to neglect the possible role that stone can play in such a scene. In a desert garden, for instance, boulders whose outlines take on stark and elegant clarity in full sun at noon will cast moody shadows later in the day, as the sun sends slanting rays across the landscape; the shade that such large stone features can provide to plants and humans in the heat of the day is indispensable. And stony dry washes, which can feature fascinating arrangements of gravel, pebbles, and rock, play a useful role after desert flash floods, because they safely channel excess surface water away from house foundations, driveways, and roads. When designed creatively, such stone features can integrate water-wise gardens with the surrounding landscape in ways that are both aesthetically pleasing and functional.

(Harry R. and Brunhilde T. Simon garden, Scottsdale, Arizona)

*A tumble of granitic boulders seems to anchor this adobe dwelling to the desert floor. Besides providing a dramatic backdrop to the stepped entryway, the boulders also serve as large-scale planters for desert natives, such as the Dr. Seuss–inspired ocotillo (*Fouquieria splendens, *right) whose shallow root system and love of well-drained soils make it a perfect candidate for a stony habitat. The garden's creator, Scottsdale designer and nurseryman George Pingitore, used massive boulders to establish a continuity of scale between the garden and house and the sweeping desert landscape in which they sit. Pingitore says that piling boulder upon boulder is so exhilarating that sometimes it's hard to gauge when to stop, so that the effect doesn't become theatrically extreme. Fortunately, his sure sense of line, shape, and proportion enables Pingitore to compose rock formations that exploit the desert's most dramatic visual effects while still looking entirely natural. (Paulette Lamoureux garden, Scottsdale, Arizona)*

Paradoxically, islands surrounded by water often lack an adequate supply of fresh water for the needs of their inhabitants. Therefore, many gardeners living on islands conserve their limited water supplies by planting water-wise gardens. Patricia Campbell wanted to make her garden, which is located on an island in Washington State's Puget Sound, resemble the nearby beach edge, with its curving ribbons of gravel, stones, and grasses carved by the actions of wind and wave. She used a variety of stones, picked up on walks along beaches and rivers throughout the state, to cover the garden floor and then added a derelict fishing boat for a focal point. The stones and gravel act as a mulch, suppressing weeds and conserving the runoff of the occasional summer rains that constitute the main source of water for the garden's drought-tolerant herbs, daylilies, and grasses. (Patricia Campbell garden, Bainbridge Island, Washington)

Bill Hays is a New Mexico garden designer who embedded locally found granite boulders in the straw-bale walls that enclose his courtyard garden. The boulders serve as dramatic focal points, providing attractive contrasts in color and texture to the mortared flags of Arizona buff sand-stone that cover the courtyard floor. In many less arid areas of the country, trees and shrubs would be used to define the boundaries of a garden room—here stone and adobe do that job, and the plants serve a decorative rather than an architectural function in the garden's design, thereby conserving precious water. (Bill Hays garden, Albuquerque, New Mexico)

This low, dry-laid stone wall of Pennsylvania bluestone provides a dramatic visual foil to a planting of water-wise, deer-resistant, and low-maintenance perennials, which was designed by garden maker Mark Douglas Oppenheimer. (Private garden, Millbrook, New York)

When Denver writer and garden designer Marcia Tatroe first decided to remove the lawn and foundation plants from her front yard in 1991, her plan was to replace them with a patio of irregular flagstone to cut down on maintenance and water use. Tatroe and her husband, Randy, selected a red sandstone for the patio flooring, placing 2-inch-thick slabs directly onto the lawn, and leaving spaces between them several inches wide, which they filled with a pink-and-gray pea gravel. After the first season, the flagstones and pea gravel had effectively suppressed the grass beneath them, and the patio was ready for planting. Originally, woolly thyme was to cover all the cracks between the flagstones, but over time, Tatroe's love of water-wise perennials, alpines, and desert species—especially those with silver, blue-green, and gray foliage—has led her to plant a much more varied palette and even to remove flagstones from the patio to give the plants more room. (Marcia and Randy Tatroe garden, Aurora, Colorado)

A fountain made of polished granite that was quarried and cut in China stands as the focal point of an entry courtyard in this Southwest garden. Smooth river cobbles, which catch water splashes at the base of the fountain, are surrounded by mortared flagstones made of Arizona rose sandstone. It may not be as dramatic as a rushing waterfall or a fountain in full flow, but the small trickle of water used in this arrangement still effectively suggests that visitors have entered a cool oasis that offers relief from the surrounding desert. (Private garden, Albuquerque, New Mexico)

Japanese garden designers traditionally make patterns in gravel beds to evoke waves and ripples in a waterless setting. Colorado gardener George Bates expands on this idea by arcing a spit of cobbles—complete with beachside flora and fauna—into a wide sea of gravel. This feature adds dramatic visual interest to an otherwise flat stretch of garden, and because the spit is planted with water-wise subshrubs and perennials, it requires little watering. (George and Vanna Bates garden, Arvada, Colorado)

Succulents tuck in between granite boulders in a Sonoran desert garden.
Arid gardens can't depend on lush masses of vegetation to achieve their
visual impact: Instead, the colors and forms of individual desert plants
take on dramatic clarity against their spare surroundings. (Harry R.
and Brunhilde T. Simon garden, Scottsdale, Arizona)

Cottage Gardens and Country Estates Cozy Charm, Rural Elegance

Say the words *English country cottage* and few American gardeners have trouble conjuring up classic images of thatched or slate roofs, casement windows, and stone or white-washed plaster walls. Similarly, it is easy to envision the traditional cottage garden as a pleasing tumble of herbs, annuals, vegetables, and roses, bisected by a flagstone path.

English cottages and cottage gardens have always been appreciated in the United States for their cozy associations and unforced charm; but when Americans set out to emulate them, we sometimes end up with entirely different animals, mainly because our building materials, construction techniques, plant palettes, and growing conditions are quite dissimilar to England's. In place of the plastered-and-thatched cottages of England's West Country, for instance, a Southwest cottage may feature smooth adobe walls and a tiled roof, whereas a Midwest cottage characteristically is built of clapboard and often has a wide wooden porch heavily encrusted with white gingerbread trim. Similarly, the water-wise plants and stony mulch in a Southwest garden and the tough, cold-hardy shrubs and flowers in a Midwest garden will each have a very different visual effect than the tender green abundance of an English cottage garden.

Both countries do, however, use stone to build cottages, as well as the walls, terraces, and paths that traditionally belong in cottage gardens. And so often it is in their use of stone that American cottage gardens most clearly reflect their English roots, especially in such features as New England's famous fieldstone walls, which remind us of the low stone walls separating the front gardens of cottages from the high street in villages throughout England. And crazy paving paths made from local stone beckon visitors through rose-wrapped garden gates as welcomingly in Denver or Dubuque as in Devonshire.

The country garden comes in all sizes and styles in England, from the large, formal grounds of a grand estate to tidy rural properties that seem only several skips larger than a cottage garden. In general, country gardens are distinguished from cottage gardens not only by being larger but also by featuring more sophisticated designs and garden structures. Many country gardens incorporate some formal elements into the overall plan, such as geometric planting beds, rectangular pools, or a series of distinct garden rooms. Like their English counterparts, the best American country gardens use axial planning to create garden vistas, include full or partial views of the surrounding countryside, and make use of sophisticated materials—especially stone.

(Vagn and Anne Jacobsen garden, Bainbridge Island, Washington)

*A cottage garden on an island in Washington
State's Puget Sound features a cozy old gazebo with
a stone chimney that is pointed with fat ribbons of
mortar for a fairy-tale effect. The granitic stones in
the chimney were picked up on local beaches by an
itinerant Polish stonemason in the 1930s, who used
the same stones and mortaring techniques throughout the garden on paths, a patio, and an outdoor
fireplace. (Vagn and Anne Jacobsen garden,
Bainbridge Island, Washington)*

*Landscape designer Ryan Gainey's
Atlanta garden mixes classic
English cottage style features—
such as the crazy paving path (made
of a regional fieldstone) that leads
straight to the garden gate—with
American folk art elements—such as
a carved and painted gate, Gothic-
style tree branch trellises, and the
potted edgings that border the path.
(Ryan Gainey garden, Atlanta,
Georgia)*

Concrete and cobblestone pillars frame a home-made wooden gate that separates the small cottage garden from the orchard; the pod of sunken cobbles scattered near the entryway functions as a subtle visual indicator that the gate is meant to bridge two distinct garden areas. (Vagn and Anne Jacobsen garden, Bainbridge Island, Washington)

American cottage gardens often demonstrate a strong regional flair, as this south Florida entry garden with its coral wall, sizzling color accents, and lush vegetation proves. (Private garden, Miami, Florida)

Garden designer R. J. Dykes III assembled cottage garden–style ornaments with a New Orleans accent—such as a painted wire bird cage, tropical potted plants, and century-old stone pavers—into a collage that brightens a corner of a courtyard in the Vieux Carre. (Soniat House Courtyard, New Orleans, Louisiana)

Petunias and lobelia spill out of a homemade flowerpot whose stone-studded surface has the same kind of unpretentious charm as the flowers it holds. Many of the farmhouses and small vacation homes on the islands in Washington State's Puget Sound were constructed just before the turn of the century, and a surprising number of them still retain their Victorian design associations. This flower container is a country cousin to the elegant mosaic-decorated containers that graced Victorian conservatories and garden terraces more than a hundred years ago. (Vagn and Anne Jacobsen garden, Bainbridge Island, Washington)

In 1923, Alfred and Elizabeth Kay purchased a large wooded estate near Chester, New Jersey, that featured an eighteenth-century farmhouse and barn built by early German immigrants. The stone used in the construction of the house and barn is a regional bedrock, which glaciers left exposed as they retreated northward, between 12,000 and 18,000 years ago. Local farmers cleared their fields of this stone by stacking it in dry-laid perimeter walls, which still line many roads surrounding Chester today; it is this hard, creamy gray stone—reminiscent of those traditionally used in Cotswold cottages and gardens—that the Kays used to construct a series of terraces, walls, and pools in their garden in the 1920s.

They were inspired by stonework in the English country gardens created around the turn of the century by architect and garden designer Sir Edwin Lutyens, whose plans characteristically integrated the house and garden into one flowing design. Lutyens's plans also typically featured several garden rooms sited around the perimeter of the estate's main residence, which usually were linked together by ornamental hardscapes, such as stone pergolas, terraces, and flights of stairs. These two concepts have continued to play key roles in the design of country gardens in England and the United States throughout this century. The Kays themselves designed most of the garden's stone features, such as this half-moon wall with a formal pool at its base. (Devereux Deerhaven, Chester, New Jersey)

This Lutyenesque sweep of granite steps leads to a terraced resting area in Penelope Maynard's large New York State garden. The blocks— roughly shaped pieces of granite saved from natural granite outcrops that were dug out of other areas in the garden—are placed with their flattest faces forward. Although mortar was used in the construction of the steps' foundations and inner core, the stonemasons withheld it from the steps' outer edges for a more natural effect. The symmetrical arrangement of ornamental pots adds a formal note to the scene. (John and Penelope Maynard garden, Bedford, New York)

A courtyard in Ryan Gainey's Georgia garden features such formal touches as mortared flagstone (made of a regional sandstone called buff Crab Orchard), a raised pool with arched architectural flourishes, and shaped evergreens in pots. (Ryan Gainey garden, Atlanta, Georgia)

Artist Hal Martin has divided his
large Midwestern country garden
into several distinct rooms by
using a series of low, dry-laid
retaining walls, which are made of
limestone rubble collected on site.
In this garden area, individual
planting beds, bordered with low
rubble walls, feature blooms and
foliage characteristic of each of the
four seasons; small stone sculptures
under trellises embellish each bed.
(Linmar Gardens, Galena,
Illinois)

Limestone strata underlie much of the landscape surrounding San Antonio, Texas; these strata provide an attractive habitat for the state's famous wildflower meadows, which display undulating waves of bluebonnets (Lupinus texensis), *Blackfoot daisies* (Melampodium leucanthum), *green thread* (Thelesperma filifolium) *and Indian blanket* (Gaillardia pulchella) *in April and May. In this country garden—which was designed to replicate aspects of a wild meadow in a more controlled setting—slabs of limestone are laid in broad ledges to act as a backdrop for a mix of native Texas wildflowers and some nonnative perennials, which extend the bloom period well into summer (Pat and Royce Caldwell garden, San Antonio, Texas)*

The sophisticated yet comfortably domestic vignette created by this carved greyhound perched on a mortared free-standing wall at Devereux Deerhaven epitomizes the particular kind of country garden style that became popular in both England and the United States during the first several decades of the twentieth century. In the previous century, garden estates often served as architectural and horticultural showpieces—and sometimes the resulting gardens were more imposing than comfortable. The movement to design more inviting, intimate spaces came about as gardeners increasingly began to use their gardens for informal entertaining and for daily family activities. (Devereux Deerhaven, Chester, New Jersey)

Water Gardens Reflections, Ripples, and Rapids

What makes a garden truly memorable? Which are the design qualities that transform a pleasing collection of plants set among pleasant surroundings into something much more—into a garden that establishes such a memorable style, presence, and atmosphere that visitors find themselves responding to it with heightened senses and an engaged imagination? And why do such memorable gardens invariably possess a water feature?

If we accept the following dictum of design—the best gardens offer visitors a multiplicity of sensory experiences—then it becomes clear why water features play such a crucial role in good garden design. No other element in a garden conveys such a rich array of simultaneous sensory experiences as a water feature does, especially one made with stone. Water as a design element is translucent, reflective, infinitely variable in pattern and texture, and makes music as it moves. Stone has directly opposite qualities: It remains silent, impervious, and immutable when displayed in a garden setting. Thus, a water feature made with stone contains a multitude of contrasting and complementary sense experiences within itself—and the union of all these elements adds up to a magical whole whose effect is greater than the sum of the parts.

(Ikune Sawada garden, eastern Washington State)

The waterfall and pond wrapping around a stuccoed building in this Santa Fe garden are constructed of stacked boulders of moss rock, a New Mexico sandstone featuring striking patinas etched by lichens and minerals. Landscape architect Catherine Clemens designed the waterfall and pond to evoke the natural water features found in the mountain landscapes of northern New Mexico; it includes two pump systems—one for the waterfall and another for the pond, with a small gravel stream running between them— providing the necessary circulation and filtration. Native iris (Iris pseudacorus) and water lilies provide shelter and shade for the fish that inhabit the pond. The dramatic and unusual juxtaposition of formal wall and informal water feature works well, in part, because the wall's stucco surface and the moss rock boulders share similar earth tones and textures. (Private garden, Santa Fe, New Mexico)

The clean, flowing lines of this informal gravel pond echo shapes found throughout the surrounding garden, which is dominated by freeform alpine meadows carved out of the foothills near Washington State's glacier-clad Mount Rainier. The pond's designer, landscape architect Rex Zumwalt, describes the resulting look as "natural but organized."

Reflecting ponds are usually formal, rectangular features, characteristic of gardens rooted in classical French, Islamic, or Italian garden traditions; this is a fine, and quite unusual, example of a natural-style reflecting pond; its edging consists of pea gravel laid on exposed aggregate, which makes it easy to clean. (Mr. and Mrs. T. E. Chase garden, Orting, Washington)

A formal raised pool lies at the center of this stone complex, which Seattle garden designer Phil Wood created for a client who wanted to fill her courtyard garden with atmospheric "ruins." The walls, arches, pool, and steps are of granite and are constructed just roughly enough to conjure up images of a crumbling classical garden that has been eroding in situ for 2,000 years. The classical motif is underscored by a wall fountain representing Bacchus and by cast concrete columns that flank the pool. (Sherri Havens garden, Bothell, Washington)

Landscape architect Tom Berger originally designed this streambed made of native Northwest granites to complement a natural-style garden. Several years later, Berger had to regrade and recontour the stream to control the destructive effects of a significantly increased water flow, which was being caused by new developments on land sited upstream. He developed a series of 3- to 4-foot-high stone steps to break the excessively fast rate of water flow and placed large boulder shoots at bends in the streambed, where erosion was most likely to occur. Through careful placement of the new stone features and by using the same types of granites, Berger was able to preserve the stream's original natural look despite its extensive redesign. (Private garden, Mercer Island, Washington)

Much of southern Florida rests on strata of limestone, the legacy of a shallow tropical sea that covered the area for millions of years before the present landforms coalesced. Because of the natural process of chemical weathering, limestone strata become brittle over time, leading to the appearance of solution holes— sudden depressions in the topography caused by the collapse of weakened limestone formations lying belowgrade.

This natural solution hole is located on the grounds of the Fairchild Tropical Garden in Miami; the original plans called for the hole to be filled in—as though it were one of nature's blemishes, to be rectified by the smoothing hand of man. But landscape architect William Lyman Phillips decided to preserve and enhance the feature by clearing it of debris; adding more rock for drama; and then planting it with an array of tropical plants, including ferns and bromeliads, that flourish among the partially decomposed surfaces of the limestone boulders. (Fairchild Tropical Garden, Miami, Florida)

Central Texas possesses scattered deposits of limestone boulders, some of which bear a remarkable
resemblance to the t'ai hu rocks that Chinese
gardeners use for their false mountains and specimen
monoliths. San Antonio landscape architect John
Troy studied Chinese water features before designing
this complex of stream, pools, and water steps that
flows between the owner's residence and a large
swimming pool at the base of the garden. The cool
white limestone and the slender twisting trunks of
the native live oaks (Quercus virginiana) give the
scene a fresh visual delicacy, which visitors find most
welcoming on a sweltering southwest afternoon.
(Limestone Creek garden, San Antonio, Texas)

Rocaille is a decorative type of
carved stonework that traditionally
adorns water features in classical
European gardens—here nature's
rocaille stands revealed in the coral
slab edging a pond in a Florida
garden. The shell-like fossil imprint
reminds us that coral, formed under
water, is the hardened accretion over
millions of years of the skeletons of
tiny marine animals. (Kenneth
Treister garden, Florida)

An intriguing water feature in a Washington State garden displays both formal and informal design elements. The granite boulder formation from which the water initially flows is naturalistic, suggesting an informal Japanese approach; but the channel below it recalls the stone water courses in classic Islamic gardens. Landscape architect Tom Berger said that the trick to getting this feature to work was adjusting the flow of water between the boulder and channel, so that it was strong enough to register a visual presence on the rock, but not to the point of then overflowing the edges of the much more constricted channel. (J. Harnall garden, Vashon Island, Washington)

This water wall is situated in a 4-foot-wide passageway that runs between a tall concrete retaining wall on one side and a house wall containing windows and a door on the other side. Landscape architect Misty Phelbin wanted to create a water feature whose sound and movement would enliven the dark passage and would be visible from the windows and doorway opposite. She decided to symbolize the natural cycle of rainfall by placing bluestone ashlar (cut stone) at the top of the wall to represent a calm and peaceful sky. Gentle sheets of rainwater fall from the ashlar sky onto the craggy mountains of bluestone rubble below; the water then collects at the bottom of the configuration to course across a riverbed made of rounded fieldstone. (Lee and Mike Brown garden, Lake Sammamish, Washington)

Patterned Gardens Pebbles, Gravels, and Mosaics

Most of the world's great gardening cultures include techniques for decorating garden floors, walls, and structures with small stones arranged in permanent or semipermanent patterns. There are practical reasons for using small pieces of stone in such garden constructions: They are durable, usually in abundant supply, and comparatively easy to transport and manipulate. But for artists, the aesthetic reasons may be paramount: The colors, textures, and shapes provide an intriguing array of possibilities for adding patterns and decorative motifs to gardens in ways that larger-scale stone constructions cannot; and garden designers have exploited such opportunities from the earliest times.

The presence of mosaics, pieced murals, patterned gravels, and other small-stone ornamentation obviates any illusions that the gardens in which they are sited are simply untouched natural landscapes; such features proclaim that the gardens are human constructs. The following photographs show how Chinese, Japanese, and Western designers have created numerous functional and aesthetic uses of small stones in gardens.

(Walker Rock Garden, Seattle, Washington)

In a Chinese courtyard, dynamic floor mosaics express the same spirited energy as the rock specimens behind them, thereby balancing and harmonizing the visual impact of the garden's floor, or horizontal plane, with its vertical features. But although the rock formations exhibit a (stylized) naturalness, the mosaics add a decidedly formal note to the garden vignette. The mosaics are composed of pebbles, roof tiles set on end, and shards of crockery that have been pressed into mortar; all of them are broken materials or leftovers from other garden projects that have been used to create a visually stunning and, at the same time, supremely practical and durable garden floor. Most Chinese floor mosaics feature abstract designs, but some depict fish, birds, bats, and other symbols of good fortune. (Dr. Sun Yat-Sen Classical Chinese Garden, Vancouver, British Columbia)

Innisfree is a large estate garden in New York State that was designed by its owner, Walter Beck, to express Chinese landscaping principles adapted to an American setting. Beck used a mix of Western-style bricks and slate medallions incised with Chinese motifs to construct a formal terrace in a hillside overlooking a large lake that forms the central feature of Innisfree. In some areas of the terrace, the bricks and slate pavers are laid out in octagons and other shapes characteristic of Chinese floor mosaics. And like many authentic Chinese mosaics, Beck's were composed from leftover materials that he used both thriftily and creatively—the bricks initially were purchased to construct a chimney; but when they turned out to be the wrong size for that project, he combined them with the slate pavers to construct the terrace. (Innisfree, Millbrook, New York)

A Western-style mural with a touch of folk art funk exhibits small stones and everyday objects set in a permanent decorative pattern. The mural was designed and installed by Brother Joseph Zoetel, who during the 1930s transformed a part of the grounds at the Benedictine Abbey of Saint Bernard in Cullman, Alabama, into a series of decorated grottoes, free-standing shrines, and miniature replicas of famous churches and basilicas from around the world. Brother Joseph used stones, shards of glass and marble, shells, costume jewelry, and small statues set in mortar to decorate his creations, which he continued to make until his death in 1961. His designs exhibit the same vigor and zest invested in everyday objects that Chinese garden mosaic work reveals. (Ave Maria Grotto, Saint Bernard Abbey, Cullman, Alabama)

These cobbles create a decorated edge between a deck and a gravel garden on a private estate in California. They also serve as a drain channel, which funnels surface water away from the foundation of the wood deck and the structure it is attached to. The arrangement of round, flat stones half-covering one another (lower center) is sometimes described by Japanese garden designers as a fish-scale pattern, and it ties in with the traditional symbolic association between gravel gardens and ocean waves. Geologists call this same pattern an imbricated structure; and it occurs naturally when flat stones are carried downstream by the force of a strong current, with their front ends rising upward and their back ends sloping downward. Wherever they come to rest in the streambed, they stack against each other in the fish-scale pattern. (Newton Vineyards, St. Helena, California)

Intricate patterns raked in a loose gravel floor surround islands in an area of the Portland Japanese Garden. Unlike the installations of small stones set in mortar featured in other gardens, these gravel patterns are impermanent and are meant to be altered over the course of time, according to the inspiration of their designers. Japanese gravel gardens originated in temple compounds and the monastic grounds of Buddhist monks by the twelfth century. They featured stones and gravel juxtaposed in mostly abstract patterns, with their positive and negative spaces meant to aid in the monks' practice of contemplation. It was usually the painstaking task of apprentices to rake new patterns into the gravel at regular intervals; the concentration and discipline needed to do the work correctly (traditionally one must accomplish it in a single continuous sweep, never lifting the rake from the ground) prepared the apprentices for the greater spiritual rigors to come. The occasional change of patterns also reminds the viewer that impermanence dominates life.

The planted islands in this gravel garden are shaped to represent a flagon and a wine bowl, symbols that imply there are numerous ways to alter reality. (Portland Japanese Garden, Portland, Oregon)

A very loose interpretation of the Japanese gravel garden concept—only the patterned waves distinguish it from a Western-style naturalistic gravel bed—provides an attractive foreground for ornamental grasses and shrubs in a woodland setting. (Anderson Gardens, Rockford, Illinois)

Designed in the 1920s by influential landscape architect Fletcher Steele as an addendum to a large 40-year-old country estate, the Naumkeag Afternoon Garden comes off as a playful art deco concoction that may be unique in the annals of sophisticated American garden design. Built as a sun trap on the west side of a 26-room mansion designed by Stanford White, the Afternoon Garden features sinuous bands of low boxwood that mark off formal parterres of pebbles and colored marble chips, four small fountains connected by a shallow reflecting pool, and carved and painted wooden pillars (originally oak pilings in Boston Harbor)—all of them helping to carry off a giddy display of designer high jinks that remains fresh and appealing 70 years later. Steele said he wanted the garden's floor to look like a richly patterned rug, implying the outside room should feel as comfortably lived in as the library/drawing room it adjoins.

    Steele's work at Naumkeag should inspire contemporary garden designers to look at the ornamental possibilities of small colored stones with new eyes, as should the colorful and vigorously flowing mosaics and murals of the very different but equally innovative landscape artist Robert Burle Marx. (Naumkeag, Stockbridge, Massachusetts)

Garden historians often note the strongly architectural qualities of Roman gardens. The continuity between the living quarters of a villa and its garden area was almost seamless: Typically the garden, or peristyle, was an interior courtyard around which the rest of the house was built. The peristyle actually functioned as an outdoor leisure room, featuring wall murals, statues, sculpted fountains, and hard floors made of stone pavement or mosaics; plants often played a minor role in such gardens, being used as decorations in much the same way as were graceful vases or bronze candelabras. (Note, however, that the Romans also had large country estates, public strolling grounds, and naturalistic seaside gardens in which plants and architectural elements played quite different roles.)

Roman garden floor mosaics were usually representational, depicting mythological events, idyllic rustic scenes, or fruits and flowers. But powerful compositions such as this series of circles and borders also explored color and line in boldly abstract patterns. (Private villa, Rome)

Italy and Spain retained and then further developed a tradition of using decorative stone patterns in garden walls and floors that was based on classical models. Portugal developed an offshoot that became the defining glory of its sixteenth-, seventeenth-, and eighteenth-century gardens—the panoramic wall decorations made of colored ceramic tiles, called azulejos, which took on a shimmering, liquid quality in the strong southern light. All three countries also used rocaille (mortared patterns of shell and pebbles) to decorate grottoes and other water features.

Northern Italy, in particular, is rich in courtyards and garden terraces that display intricate stone floors. This courtyard in the small town of Santa Margherita Ligure, near Genoa, features a mortared pebble floor patterned with floral arabesques that are reminiscent of the parterres popular in classical French gardens of the seventeenth century. Combined with the classical-style oil jars and statues that flank the villa, the scene shows how masterfully the Italians can blend various garden features and ornaments developed over centuries into a single vignette. (Private garden, Santa Margherita Ligure, Italy)

habitats

Stone plays a crucial role in the generation and distribution of plant and animal life on earth. The decomposition of mineral-rich stone underlying the ancient oceans of the pre-Proterozoic eras helped trigger the habitat conditions necessary for the appearance of the first aquatic microbes almost three billion years ago. By 600 million years ago, the microbes had evolved into multicelled aquatic plants, most of them algae, and multicelled aquatic animals, such as sponges, corals, and jellyfish. The animal life further developed into bony fishes and amphibians, some of which, migrating onto land in the Devonian era (400 to 350 million years ago), became the ancestors of the reptiles, birds, and mammals that inhabit the earth today.

Plants, mainly simple nucleated algae, had migrated from the oceans onto land earlier than did animals, in the late Silurian to early Devonian era (440 to 400 million years ago), where they first evolved into mosses and liverworts. Stone formations provided the new land plants with habitat conditions that allowed them to evolve, diversify, and spread across the face of the earth. Because different types of rock formations influence a wide range of habitat conditions—from the macroweather patterns associated with mountain chains to the composition of a pocket of soil in a single rocky outcrop—stone has played a determining role in the spread of plants and the consequent appearance of the landscape itself. Today the angiosperms, or flowering plants, dominate the terrestrial plant kingdom, but many gardeners still get a frisson whenever they see a planting arrangement of mosses and ferns—some of earth's few remaining primitive plants—nestled up to their ancient nurturers and protectors, the stones. It's a scene that was old well before dinosaurs roamed the earth.

Although it was botanists and geologists who first studied the ecological relationships between plants and stones, gardeners became interested in using stone as a habitat for plants—rather than merely as a decorative setting for them—by the late nineteenth and early twentieth centuries, when growing alpine plants became a craze among British and American gardeners. As they studied the growing conditions of alpine plants in natural mountain settings, these gardeners began to replicate the same features (stony outcrops, fissures, and screes) in their gardens. More recently, rock gardeners are beginning to recreate all kinds of natural land-scapes featuring stone, not just mountain scenes. Meadows, beaches, and woodland ravines are some of the settings in which gardeners now use rock and stones as plant habitats. The plants recommended in the sections that follow were selected because they are particularly suited for the habitat under discussion, will do well in most U.S. plant hardiness zones, and are comparatively easy to find at nurseries or in plant catalogs.

Gardeners have come to value gardens that incorporate stone features not only as superlative environments for growing alpine and other rock plants but also as aesthetically pleasing landscapes with their own distinctive styles. Public gardens featuring natural-looking stone formations, such as Washington State's Ohme Gardens in Wenatchee and Chase Garden in Orton, New Jersey's Leonard J. Buck Garden in Far Hills, Colorado's Betty Ford Alpine Gardens in Vail and the rock gardens at the Denver Botanical Gardens, and New York's Botanical Garden, best show the delicate and profound art of combining stone and plants into a thriving habitat.

(Denver Botanical Gardens)

Fissures

*Fissures are vertical cracks or breaks in rock; often they start
as fractures created by earthquakes, and then become wider
and deeper as erosion takes its toll. They create an excellent
habitat for rock plants, provided their openings are wide
enough and deep enough to hold the amount of soil necessary
for adequate root growth. The deeper reaches of the fissure
should have small stones and pebbles mixed with the soil to
ensure sharp drainage.*

*Some rock gardeners create artificial fissures by
vertically stacking small pieces of stone between two larger
rocks at the point at which they lie closest together.
Gardeners then fill in the remaining areas between the
cracks with soil. Such artificial fissures soften the sometimes
awkward-looking meeting points between rocks that have
been placed next to each other in a constructed stonescape.*

*This garden fissure is constructed from a Pacific
Northwest native basalt that breaks into flat sheets with
flaky edges, which gardeners Ernie and Marietta O'Byrne
gleaned from an abandoned quarry near their home in
Eugene, Oregon. Normally, sedimentary stones such as limestone and sandstone are recommended for rock gardens—
not only are they soft enough for easy shaping but their
weather-worn surfaces give a settled-in look to even newly
constructed rock formations. In addition, sedimentary stones
are porous and water retentive, allowing excess moisture in
the surrounding soil to wick away rapidly from plant
roots, and yet remain available as a source of moisture
when required.*

*Igneous and metamorphic rock, including granite,
basalt, and gneiss, are traditionally considered less desirable
for rock gardening because they are harder to shape, often
have raw, sharp edges, and are of a dense, less-porous
texture. But because rock gardeners in all parts of the country
consistently report good results from using local igneous and
metamorphic rock, new rock gardeners might well consider
using these alternatives if these materials are less expensive
and easier to procure than sedimentary rock. As always,
consult local rock gardeners about their favorite types of rock
for building and for the plants they recommend for specific
stone habitats. (Ernie and Marietta O'Byrne garden,
Eugene, Oregon)*

Plants for Fissures

Most of the plants listed here are compact and have roots
that tolerate constricted growing space. Varieties with long
periods of bloom have been emphasized.

Androsace lanuginosa (rock jasmine)
Light pink flowers form over clumps of narrow dusty green foliage in
middle to late summer. Tolerates full sun to high shade; requires
fast-draining soil.

Draba aizoides
Delicate yellow flowers on wiry stems bloom in spring above cushiony
evergreen foliage. Likes sun and fast-draining soil.

Lewisia cotyledon (Siskiyou bitterroot)
Hot pink or orange flowers bloom in early summer above succulent,
strappy leaves. Requires well-drained soil, sun only in the morning in
hot climates, and protection from standing water on the leaves and
crown.

Omphalodes luciliae
Loose clusters of blue flowers above bluish green leaves in midsummer.
Likes a sunny position, nutrient-poor soil, and a gravel mulch.

Penstemon rupicola (beardtongue)
Tubular bright red flowers rise above dense, shrubby foliage. Requires
sun, shelter from wind, and fast-draining soil.

Primula marginata hybrids (rockery primroses)
Violet to sky blue blooms grace the cream-margined leaves of these
small, early-flowering varieties. Likes light shade and a nonclayey but
nondry soil.

Saxifraga kabschia (cushion saxifrage)
Early-blooming varieties have hummocky mats of silver and gray
leaves. Requires fast-draining soil that never completely dries out,
partial shade, and a gritty mulch composed of stone particles.

Sedum cauticola (stonecrop)
Clusters of deep pink flowers appear late in the growing season carried
on the 6-inch-high blue-green, narrow leaves of this trailing succulent;
remains evergreen in milder climates. Easy to grow; tolerates sun or
light shade, nutrient-poor (and fast-draining) soil, and some drought.

Viola labradorica (rockery violet)
Fresh, light purple flowers are featured on delicate, purple-blue leaves
in the spring. Tolerates filtered sun and light shade in any well-drained
soil; looks especially attractive crawling down a fissure.

Screees

Screes are slopes of loose gravel and rock fragments that fan out from the base of cliffs or stony outcrops; in the natural landscape, they often support a wide variety of alpine and rock plants because they offer gritty soils with excellent drainage. In the garden, even screes that are constructed without large stones or a pronounced slope can act as effective habitats for the same range of plants: It is the presence of fast-draining soil and several inches of gravelly mulch that creates the necessary growing conditions for successful scree gardening.

The mulch in this scree garden is a mix of pumice, cinders, and open gravel 1/4-inch or larger. (Open gravel has no added fillers or binders that could pack down and prevent quick water drainage. Granite and limestone chips also make good open scree coverings.) The mulch has been laid down over a soil especially blended for alpine and rock plants: The classic mix is equal parts of humus, loam, and gravel or grit; but each gardener will vary the proportions for individual plants and growing conditions as experience dictates.

Randomly embedded pieces of basalt add contrasting form and texture to the gravelly mix, and a dwarf conifer near the summit adds height to the bed, while visually integrating it with the rest of the garden. Screes are often designed as intermediary features that are meant to join together topographically distinct areas of a garden, such as an open meadow and a large outcrop. (Ernie and Marietta O'Byrne garden, Eugene, Oregon)

Plants for Screes

The majority of plants listed here enjoy open, sunny exposures and flourish in a gritty mulch.

Armeria maritima (sea thrift)
Clustered pink, crimson, or white flowers bloom in midsummer over strappy mounds of foliage; a hardy sun-lover. Requires well-drained soil.

Asperula gussonii (alpine woodruff)
Light pink flowers are carried on low, matting foliage in mid-spring. Tolerates full sun to light shade; requires fast-draining, acid soil.

Campanula garganica (bellflower)
Deep blue stars bloom in summer over a mat of tender, fresh green leaves. Likes full sun and light soil.

Dianthus pavonius (rockery pink)
Bright pink flowers with tan undersides bloom middle to late summer over evergreen leaves. Needs full sun and very good drainage.

Erodium corsicum (cranesbill)
Delicate pink blooms top gray lobed and ribbed leaves in June and July. Tolerates most fast-draining garden soils; requires a sunny exposure.

Gentiana septemfida (gentian)
Bell-shaped blue flowers bloom in midsummer over dense evergreen leaves. Likes rich, fast-draining soil and an open, sunny position.

Gypsophila repens (creeping baby's breath)
Pink or white masses of tiny flowers bloom over silvery foliage in midsummer. Requires full sun and light soil; responds well to a dressing of lime in spring.

Leontopodium alpinum (edelweiss)
Fresh white blooms appear on narrow gray-green leaves in June and July. Needs full sun and moist, fast-draining soil. Most attractive if planted in clumps hugging hillsides, as in their native Alps.

Phlox douglasii (alpine phlox)
Summer blooms, ranging from red to white and purple, adorn spreading clumps of foliage. Requires full sun and moist but not soggy soil.

Silene schafta (rock campion)
Bright purple-red flowers bloom in late summer over a dense mat of leaves. Likes an open, sunny spot and a light, dry soil.

Ledges

Thoughtfully designed and constructed ledges can be among the most attractive and useful stone formations to add to a rock garden. Because the horizontal layers of a ledge formation step back in natural-looking terraces with plenty of room for pockets of soil between them, plants that have long taproots and foliage that likes to sprawl over a dry, warm surface do especially well in a ledge habitat.

If the ledge is constructed so that the stones tilt downward toward the back, then rainwater will be directed to the plant roots, and the site will get the maximum sun exposure possible during the course of the day. Some gardeners enjoy constructing two ledge formations that face each other, with a gravel path winding between them like a dry stream bed in the floor of an arroyo or ravine. Such an arrangement allows the rock gardener to experiment with many plants that need different kinds of light exposures and soil conditions. (Denver Botanic Gardens, Denver, Colorado)

Plants for Ledges

The plants in this list do especially well in ledge habitats; many of the plants listed in the outcrops section on page 107, can also be considered for ledge habitats.

Arabis ferdinandi-coburgi 'Variegata' (variegated rock cress)
Although the spring-flowering white blooms are handsome, the evergreen leaves with their fresh, white margins are the main attraction. Very hardy and easy to grow; requires full sun and well-draining soil.

Aubrieta deltoidea (purple rock cress)
Starry mauve flowers bloom in late spring against evergreen mats of deep green leaves. Likes full sun and well-draining soil; considered long living and disease resistant.

Oenothera acaulis (evening primrose)
Large, white cup-shaped flowers appear above lush leaves that like to crawl across rock surfaces. Thrives in light but moist soil and full sun.

Phlox subulata (moss-pink)
Named varieties and hybrids have blooms ranging in color from white to pink and red over cushion foliage. Likes a very lean soil and a sunny, open site.

Saponaria ocymoides (soapwort)
Summer-blooming rosy flowers appear over the many-leafed stems of this sprawling, floriferous plant. Likes a gritty, well-drained soil and plenty of sun.

Thymus membranaceous (Spanish thyme)
Unusually large white flowers over a dwarf bush form. Likes excellent drainage and full sun.

Outcrops

Outcrops are the parts of a stone formation that appear above the surface of the earth; like icebergs, they usually constitute a small percentage of the total mass of the formations, most of which remain below the surface and out of sight. It is that sense of hidden monumentality that a rock gardener seeks to replicate in constructing an artificial outcrop. (Outcrops differ from ledges in appearance, because although ledges seem to retreat into a hillside, outcrops seem to jut out from it. Consequently, ledges tend to appear restful to the eye, whereas outcrops often look more dramatic.)

Many gardeners work with natural outcrops, which they can enlarge either by exposing more of the formation that was originally lying belowground or by incorporating new rocks into the original feature. If rock is added, it should be of the same type as the original and similarly weathered. In addition, the new rock should be positioned at the same angle as the original formation, so it looks like the entire outcrop, old and new, has experienced the same natural geological events, such as earthquake, upheaval, or erosion, at the same point in time. (Ohme Gardens, Wenatchee, Washington)

Plants for Outcrops

The plants listed here range in size from compact specimens to sprawling subshrubs; varieties with evergreen or semievergreen foliage have been emphasized.

Arenaria montana (mountain sandwort)
Small white blooms cover evergreen mats of foliage in late spring. Requires a sunny position and moist soil.

Calluna (heather)
Late summer blooms appear on evergreen subshrubs that range in height from a few inches to 2^{1}/$_{2}$ feet. Requires full sun and an acid soil.

Diascia (twinspur)
Delicate rosy blooms nod above the matting foliage for several months. Thrives in a sunny exposure and fast-draining soil.

Helianthemum nummularium (rockrose)
Long-lasting summer blooms in a variety of colors cover evergreen leaves; after the first bloom, prune hard to encourage season-long flowering. Requires well-drained soil and a sunny position.

Iberis sempervirens (candytuft)
Long-lasting white blooms smother attractive evergreen leaves in late spring. Flourishes in general garden soil; tolerates sun to light shade.

Oenothera missouriensis (Missouri evening primrose)
Sprawling, cup-shaped yellow flowers open as the sun loses force in the evening. Requires sandy moist soil and full sun.

Origanum vulgare 'Aureum' (rockery marjoram)
Shrubby gold foliage and a compact growth habit. Thrives in fast-draining soil and full sun.

Paoulia australis (scabweed)
This low, silvery gray groundcover looks very appealing crawling along a stone, hugging its surface as closely as a velvet glove fits a hand. Requires a mild winter climate, lots of sun, and very well-drained soil.

Meadows

Natural-looking meadows are among the hardest of habitats to keep looking fresh and filled in, because many of the plants traditionally used in them have short flowering periods, mostly in spring, and rather undistinguished foliage. However, they are not particularly hard to construct if you have the right setting, which is a good sweep of land open to sun and air. First, dig over the soil to a depth of at least 18 inches, removing weeds and other unwanted plants—roots and all—and then amend it with rock particles, pumice, or other ingredients that promote fast drainage. Finally, add some compost or chopped leaves for enrichment. If you place a few horizontal rocks with gently rounded crowns (of the type Japanese gardeners sometimes refer to as the reclining ox) in the meadow, they will provide some visual interest and also a habitat for plants that like to tuck their roots into the cool, moist soils existing underneath stone.

Meadows can host a large variety of plants, from grasses, groundcovers, and bulbs to wildflowers; but getting the mix right—so invasive plants don't overwhelm the more delicate kinds and so that there is a lively succession of color and texture throughout the growing season—calls for thoughtful planting. This Pacific Northwest meadow scene features a sophisticated palette of alpines and rock and meadow plants; in mid-spring, sweeps of the native-flowering bulb Erythronium *(its different varieties have evocative common names, such as the fawn lily and dog-tooth violet) carpet the meadow, which lies near the foothills surrounding snowcapped Mount Rainier. (Mr. and Mrs. T. E. Chase garden, Orting, Washington)*

Plants for Meadows

Using a preponderance of groundcovers that continue to look good after bloom may be the key to successfully planting a meadow—many varieties of low phloxes, rock cresses, thymes, bugleweeds, and thrifts will serve well in this role. Some noninvasive grasses and dwarf conifers, spiked with colorful clumps of poppies and wildflowers can put the finishing touches on the meadow tapestry effect.

Ajuga (bugleweed)
Spiky flowers appear above the plump, shiny leaves of this low groundcover in middle to late spring. Looks best when planted in masses and drifts; cut off spent blooms and keep well watered to ensure fresh and appealing fall foliage. Tolerates sun and shade; likes well-drained soil that never completely dries out. Invasive.

Arabis caucasica (rock cress)
Frothy white flowers bloom above gray-green mats of foliage in late spring. Tolerates sun or high shade; requires well-drained soil.

Arctostaphylos uva-ursi (kinnikinnick)
Pink flowers appear above the shiny, attractive leaves of this evergreen creeper in spring. Tolerates sun to light shade; requires lime-free soil.

Artemisia caucasica (silver artemisia)
Bright yellow blooms contrast with the delicate, silvery foliage of this low spreader. Very hardy; requires only sun and fast-draining soil.

Astilbe chinensis 'Pumila' (rockery astilbe)
Deep pink feathery plumes last from midsummer through fall; much lower than common border astilbes. Requires moist soil; tolerates high shade.

Briza media (quaking grass)
Compact, noninvasive grass with attractive seed heads. Responds well to full sun and fast-draining soil.

Crocus speciosus (autumn crocus)
White, rose, or purple cup-shaped flowers in August through October. Likes full sun and fast-draining soil.

Daphne cneorum (dwarf daphne)
Fragrant rosy blooms cluster above evergreen foliage in mid-spring. Thrives in sunny but not baking exposure; likes rich, well-drained soil.

Liriope muscari (lilyturf)
Spiky white or purple blooms above thick tufts of evergreen grasslike leaves in late summer. Tolerates sun or shade and regular garden soil.

Narcissus bulbocodium (hoop-petticoat daffodil)
A dwarf with charming bright yellow blooms in mid-spring; the dying foliage is less noticeable than that of many other types. Requires well-drained soil and full sun.

Papaver alpinum (alpine poppy)
A dwarf with yellow, pink, orange, or white blooms in midsummer. Likes gravelly soil and full sun.

Potentilla x tonguei (rock cinquefoil)
Orange flowers bloom over low, evergreen mats of foliage. Likes full sun and fast-draining soil.

Pulsatilla vernalis (pasque flower)
Silky white blooms touched with purple appear at Eastertime. Delicate, divided leaves support seed heads in late summer and fall. Likes limey, fast-draining soil and plenty of sun.

Sisyrinchium californicum (yellow-eyed grass)
Cheerful yellow flowers sported on spearlike leaves bloom intermittently throughout the growing season. Requires full sun and a rich, moist soil.

Thymus serpyllum (creeping thyme)
White, red, or pink blooms in early summer on large mats that act as an attractive carpet on the meadow garden floor. Thrives in an open sunny position and well-drained soil.

Woodlands

Many gardeners live in regions of the country where forests are (or, increasingly, were) the dominant type of landscape. Some of these natural forest settings feature rocky outcrops or stony hillsides where ferns and other shade-loving woodland natives find a highly congenial home. Gardeners who want to replicate forest settings and those who want to exploit the full ornamental possibilities of an already existing natural woodland garden can use stone features as visually attractive design elements in many different ways because stones reflect the play of sun and shadow, show off patterns of mosses and lichens etched across their surfaces, and gently channel raindrops falling from the overhanging trees to the groundcovers below. And as habitats, stone features help provide the conditions of shelter and shade that woodland plants typically need to flourish. (Jane Platt garden, Portland, Oregon)

Plants for Woodlands

Along with rhododendrons, azaleas, ferns, and mosses, the following plants do well in a rocky woodland setting.

Cyclamen hederifolium (hardy cyclamen)
Rosy pink flowers bloom in late summer over the marbled leaves of this delicate shade lover. Likes a well-drained but rich woodland soil.

Daphne blagayana
The creamy flowers of this evergreen shrublet bloom in the spring. Roots require winter protection; likes sun to high shade and a rich soil well-amended with chopped leaves.

Epimedium (barrenwort)
The blooms of this groundcover range from yellows to creams, whites, and reds and contrast with the delicate deciduous to semievergreen leaves. Likes high shade and well-drained soil.

Hepatica americana
Delicate light purple flowers look attractive tumbling down a rocky hillside; one of the earliest woodland plants to bloom. Requires a fast-draining soil that remains constantly moist and light shade.

Pieris japonica (lily-of-the-valley shrub)
Clusters of bell-like flowers appear on this large evergreen shrub with shiny narrow leaves. Thrives in high shade and a well-drained acid soil.

Sanguinaria canadensis (bloodroot)
Startling white blooms appear in early spring before the heavily textured foliage unfolds; small plant with lots of woodland character. Needs a rich, acid soil and light shade.

Trillium grandiflorum
An elegantly triangular flower in shades of mauve, yellow, white, and chocolate bloom above this small, deciduous trileafed woodland plant. Thrives in shade and rich, fast-draining soils.

Gravel

As a garden mulch, gravel provides a pleasing neutral background against which the foliage and blooms of plants take on special clarity of form and color. Or you can deliberately coordinate the color schemes of the gravel with the plants: Gravel comes in shades running from creams and browns to blues and grays, making it possible to find or mix gravel to suit every combination of foliage and blooms. Use gravels that are no more than 5/8 inch in diameter; placed 1 to 1 1/2 inches thick over a soil that has previously been weeded and amended, gravel discourages further weed growth, conserves moisture, and keeps rain and mud from splashing up onto plants. Burying soaker hoses in gravel creates an inexpensive, water-conserving irrigation system that may be rerouted as needed with little trouble. (Kay D. Galvan garden, Denver, Colorado)

Plants for Gravel

Gravel is a particularly attractive and useful habitat in which to grow the following kinds of water-wise plants, wildflowers, and self-seeding annuals and perennials.

Alchemilla mollis (lady's mantle)
If the early summer yellow blooms are cut off after flowering, the pretty, pleated foliage of this self-seeder will look fresh most of the growing season. Tolerates sun to light shade and general garden soil.

Achillea filipendulina (fern-leaf yarrow)
Tiny yellow flowers in flat corymbs appear on this tall plant with delicate gray-green foliage; not a self-seeder. Likes sun and sharp drainage.

Allium flavum (flowering onion)
The bright yellow blooms of this prolific self-seeder stand 9–12 inches high. Likes fast-draining soil and an open, sunny position.

Artemesia lanata
Yellow flowers bloom in summer over silvery leaves. Likes sun and very well drained soil; needs protection from winter wet.

Echinops ritro 'Veitch's Blue' (globe thistle)
Intense blue, globe-shaped flowers top this tall, architectural plant with crinkly leaves. Likes full sun and well-drained soil.

Helichrysum lanatum
Silver felt deciduous leaves are the main attraction, providing a good season-long complement to the vivid blooms of the other plants listed here. Thrives with sharp drainage, a sheltered position, and full sun.

Lavandula officinalis nana (lavender)
Long-lasting spikes of bright lavender-blue flowers bloom above the gray-green leaves of this compact shrub. Likes full sun and a light soil.

Penstemon hartwegii (garden penstemon)
Showy white, purple, red, or pink tubular blooms grace this shrubby perennial. Likes a fast-draining soil and plenty of sun.

Tanacetum vulgare (tansy)
Small yellow flowers are attractively set off by the fresh green ferny leaves. Likes sunny exposure and well-drained soil.

Verbascum bombyciferum (mullein)
Bright yellow flowers on candelabra spires appear in midsummer above the large, felty, dusty green leaves of this stately biennial; a prolific self-seeder. Likes plenty of sun and a gravelly mulch.

Beaches

Stones half-buried in sandy soil at water's edge create a picturesque habitat for the grasses and groundcovers that thrive in a beach environment. Stones and boulders are often placed on a beach to break wave action and to slow the process of erosion; but if they are arranged in a pleasing design and "planted" thoughtfully, they can serve to extend the atmospherics of the beach or lakeside farther up into the rest of the garden. (John W. Reynolds garden, Hood Canal, Washington)

Plants for Beaches

In addition to native beach grasses and groundcovers that thrive near the water's edge in your area, these trees and shrubs tolerate the sandy soil and windy conditions often found at a beach environment. Because these plants don't like to have wet feet, they should be planted in the no-man's-land between beach and garden, or the area where the beach ends and the soils and watering conditions of the normal garden environment begin.

Arbutus unedo (strawberry tree)
Dimpled orangey-red fall fruits are produced on this small, shaggy tree with shiny evergreen leaves; attractive twisting trunks with peeling cocoa brown bark.

Cytisus scoparius (common broom)
Clusters of flowers appear in late spring on this fountain-shaped shrub with arching, spiny twigs.

Lavatera (bush mallow)
The blooms of this deciduous shrub possess the unusual merit of being shatterproof, even in brisk sea breezes; long flowering season.

Pinus mugo (mugo pine)
Attractive low, spreading evergreen pine with springy, upright needles; a good spreader and mounder that serves as an attractive backdrop for flowering groundcovers.

Potentilla fruticosa (shrubby cinquefoil)
Cheerful late spring flowers, available in a variety of colors, adorn this mid-size deciduous shrub.

Rosa rugosa
The long succession of blooms on this tough shrub introduce fragrance to the seaside garden. Not fussy about growing conditions.

Wetlands

Wetlands play an important ecological role by absorbing and filtering rain and groundwater and by providing habitat for plants, fish, animals, and insects. Gardeners also value them as beautifully subtle and atmospheric settings for unstructured water gardens. Stones can be used in these gardens in a variety of ways: for example, as ornamental barriers between bog areas and adjacent ponds and as natural stepping-stones across water. They also serve as convenient sunning spots for turtles and snakes, while shallow depressions in their crowns can be used as watering holes for birds and butterflies. In addition, the undersides of stones that have been cantilevered over the water provide valuable shelter and shade for fish and amphibians. In this Northwest garden, granite boulders from the Cascade Mountains form a natural-looking boundary between a large ornamental pond, which is sited above them, and the settling pond, which sits below them. (Mr. and Mrs. Probst garden, Redmond, Washington)

Plants for Wetlands

A lush waterside planting featuring both horizontal and vertical accents softens the edges between a wetlands and its surrounding landscape.

Cornus stolonifera 'Flaviramea' (yellow-twig dogwood)
The lemon yellow twigs of this mid-size deciduous shrub sing out against a gray winter sky. Tolerates wet soil; thrives in sunny to semi-shadey conditions.

Iris kaempferi (Japanese iris)
Elegant purple blooms are held above delicate leaves in early summer; disease resistant and low maintenance. Can be planted in shallow water; likes sun.

Osmunda regalis (royal fern)
Delicate arching fronds turn fiery orange in the fall. Likes moist soil and high shade.

Petasites japonicus (Japanese butterbur)
Yellow flowers contrast with the lush, large, rounded leaves in spring. Likes wet soil and high shade.

Primula pulverulenta (bog primrose)
Deep wine blooms with purple eyes stand a foot above the ribbed foliage. Prefers moist but not consistently wet soil.

Typha angustifolia (cattails)
Velvety brown inflorescences surmount 6-foot-tall narrow spears; dramatic vertical accent. Likes to stand in water in full sun.

Troughs

When gardeners first started growing alpines in a garden setting, they frequently had trouble acclimatizing these mountain natives to lowland climates and soils. As a result, ingenious gardeners began to create rock gardens, screes, and other large-scale features in their own backyards to provide the alpines with a controlled environment that more or less replicated the mountain conditions in which such plants naturally grow. Stone troughs provide yet another kind of habitat for alpines, rock plants, and dwarf conifers—one that is small in scale, readily moveable, and ornamental. In addition, gardeners can easily micromanage a trough's soils, watering schedule, and exposure to create the growing conditions really fussy plants need.

Rock gardeners often cluster troughs of varying sizes and shapes together as a focal point in the garden. Authentic stone troughs are difficult to procure in the United States, but hypertufa (a mixture of sand, peat moss, and cement) can be molded to make excellent substitutes. (Ernie and Marietta O'Byrne garden, Eugene, Oregon)

Plants for Troughs

Most the plants listed here have a long bloom period, which makes them especially useful subjects for a trough arrangement.

Armeria juniperfolia (dwarf thrift)
Rosy pink or cream flowers appear above gray-green spiky foliage that reaches 3 inches high. Requires full sun and well-drained soil.

Erinus alpinus (fairy foxglove)
Starry pink flowers bloom spring through summer above clumping deep green leaves that stand 4 inches high. Prefers sun to partial shade and light soil.

Erodium reichardii 'Album'
Long-lived white flowers appear in summer above attractive leaves; compact plant. Requires full sun and well-drained soil.

Rhodohypoxis baurii
Cheerful, long-lived purple, white, or pink multipetaled blooms stand about 2 inches high above crocus-like leaves. Needs full sun and well-drained soil.

Saponaria x *olivana* (soapwort)
Tiny clusters of deep pink flowers bloom above a dense mat of bright green leaves. Likes full sun and a stony mulch.

Deserts

As the arid regions of the West become increasingly populated, American gardeners are encountering a whole new range of plants—desert natives—that have their own special design possibilities and cultural requirements.

Most arid-country gardeners in the United States live in one of the four major desert environments that stretch across the American Southwest: the Sonoran, Chihuahuan, Mojave, and California–Colorado deserts. Although the deserts differ in climate, elevation, topography, and plant palette, they share some common characteristics, including extreme heat and low rainfall for much of the year; soil that is generally gravelly or sandy, alkaline, and fast draining; and communities of plants that have evolved to flourish in these kinds of conditions. (Harry R. and Brunhilde T. Simon garden, Scottsdale, Arizona)

Plants for Deserts

The following plants—including trees, shrubs, perennials, and groundcovers—successfully adapt to a range of arid Southwest environments, even though originally they may have been native to only one area. Most of them (with exceptions noted) tolerate dry, sandy soils and require minimal or no watering, once their roots are comfortably established.

Acacia baileyana (Bailey acacia)
Scented yellow flowers and fernlike, divided leaves adorn this small, multi-trunked tree; provides a light shade for groundcovers.

Agave neomexicana
(New Mexico agave)
Sharply defined dusty green leaves outlined in black and culminating in shiny black tips; signature plant for the desert garden.

Berlandiera lyrata (chocolate daisy)
Attractive wildflower with a rich chocolate fragrance; cultivate near a patio or entryway.

Celtis reticulata (palo blanco)
Long-lived shade tree that remains compact enough in usual desert growing conditions not to overwhelm a small garden; provides shelter and berries for birds.

Cercidium floridum
(blue palo verde)
Yellow flowers, which bloom in early spring, appear on the delicate, twisting branches of this small, multitrunked tree; makes a lovely silhouette against the sky; blooms attract bees

Choisya dumosa
(starleaf Mexican orange)
White flowers appear on this fragrant shrub that smells of oranges. Requires some shade in very hot environments.

Dalea gregii (trailing indigo bush)
In the spring, lavender blooms contrast with the silver-gray foliage of this groundcover; small, shrublike, mounding habit.

Fouquieria splendens (ocotillo)
Flaming orange-red blooms top spiny, twisty stems (that reach 10–20 feet high) in the spring; wild man of the desert.

Larrea tridentata (creosote bush)
Small yellow flowers bloom intermittently year-round on this multitrunked evergreen shrub; releases a pungently distinctive scent after a rain.

Muhlenbergia rigens (deergrass)
A medium-size grass that provides year-round structure; works especially nicely as the backdrop for ephemeral wildflowers.

Nolina longifolia
(Mexican grasstree)
Shining leaves grow quickly on this spiky, evergreen grass; eventually develops an attractively twisting trunk.

Penstemon eatonii
(Eaton's penstemon)
Tubular, spring-blooming, rosy red flowers complement gray evergreen leaves that clamber up a prominent stalk; blooms attract birds and butterflies.

Prosopis glandulosa
(Texas mesquite)
Yellow flowers appear in the spring on the spreading branches of this small tree with shaggy bark; fresh green leaves provide light shade.

Sphaeralcea ambigua
(desert mallow)
Spring flowers in shades of pink and cream cluster along stems contrasting with the spikey, dusty-green leaves; perennial.

Paving

Paving is perhaps the most ubiquitous special environment to be found in a garden. Plants are usually placed between individual pavers in a terrace or along the borders of paths to soften their hard edges; the interplay between the soft organic forms and textures of the plants and the sharply contrasting qualities of the paving materials can become an attractive design element in almost any garden setting. Stone, especially, provides a dramatic foil to plants featuring a wide variety of textures, colors, and forms. (Marcia and Randy Tatroe garden, Aurora, Colorado)

Plants for Paving

Most of the plants listed here will tolerate at least moderate foot traffic; exceptions are noted.

Acaena buchananii (sheep bur)
Small, decorative, deep yellow burrs top mats of dusty green foliage in summer. Needs some protection from a baking sun; likes fast-draining but moist soil.

Alyssum montanum
Thickly clustered cheerful yellow flowers cover the low evergreen foliage in late spring. Takes sun or high shade; requires a well-drained soil.

Antennaria dioica (pussy toes)
Soft pink blooms appear above short, woolly mats of foliage in spring. Likes sun and well-drained soil.

Anthemis nobilis (common chamomile)
Short tufty groundcover; a natural spreader that releases a fresh scent when bruised by foot traffic. Tolerates a hot, dry site.

Lychnis alpina (dwarf campion)
Long-lasting pink flowers cover low foliage from May to July. Needs fertile soil that remains on the dry side and full sun. Avoid foot traffic.

Veronica prostrata 'Rosea' (rock speedwell)
Showy, long-lasting pink blooms cover small mounds of springy foliage in early summer. Likes fertile, dry soil and sun or high shade.

The following plants also flourish in paving.

Arenaria montana (page 107)

Aubrieta deltoidea (page 105)

Campanula garganica (page 103)

Omphalodes luciliae (page 101)

Raoulia australis (page 107)

Saponaria ocymoides (page 105)

Powerful Stones

About ten thousand years ago, hunters near present-day Jinmium in Western Australia pecked out hundreds of dotted patterns and designs on stone outcrops standing near the mouth of a large complex of caves. The patterns engraved on the rocks are mostly abstract (although one closely resembles that immemorial Australian icon, the kangaroo). Archaeologists theorize that the rock art was created to mark the caves as spiritually significant sites for these early humans, who most probably used them to conduct religious rites.

Because of its durability and ubiquity, stone is the material from which most prehistoric works were made—at least this is true of most of the ancient artwork that has come down to us today. Artistically powerful paintings of horses, bison, mammoths, and bears, for instance, were drawn on the limestone walls of caves in southwestern France, northern Spain, and northeastern Portugal well over thirty thousand years ago. These "action art" pieces, colored with coal and mineral-rich clays and mud, were possibly used in an attempt to channel the animals' spirits and energy into the painters, to make them better hunters. (Current arguments over whether the cave painters had purely spiritual or purely pragmatic motivations

for drawing the animals seem quite beside the point—surely for people living on such a thin margin of survival, hunting *was* holy work.) At roughly the same time, three-inch-high limestone figures depicting human females, their pendulous hips and thighs symbolizing a magically inexhaustible fecundity, were being carved in central Europe. Thus, there is evidence that the very earliest stone art we know of possessed a spiritual and/or magical significance for its creators.

The use of stone to create symbols of spiritual power continues down through history and in many cultures, from "magic bundles" of stones found in cave settlements in northern Europe to the vast stone temples in ancient Egypt, the Middle East, and Central America that embody the beliefs and aspirations of their societies in constructions meant to last forever. In China, jade was considered a chip of the immortal heavens fallen to earth, and Han Dynasty emperors (206 B.C.–A.D. 220), in a bid for eternal preservation, were clad in burial suits made of hundreds of jade pieces held together with gold thread. The pre-Columbian Maya culture conferred spiritual power on the same stone—a burial mask of jade platelets covered the

(The Owenses garden, Bainbridge Island, Washington)

127

face of Lord Pacal, a seventh-century leader of the jungle city-state of Palenque, the limestone ruins of which are located in the lowland jungles of Mexico's Chiapas State. Today, the descendants of Pacal's subjects still believe that supernatural jaguars who prowl the night jungles turn into boulders each morning, as soon as the sun's first rays reach the forest floor. Historically, native Hawaiians used special monoliths to represent gods, or the power of gods; they also piled up volcanic stones as platforms for their open-air temples, or *heiaus*, where they left offerings, wrapped in ti leaves and wedged into niches in the rubble walls, to the gods. Many modern island families still possess specimen stones to which they feel powerful emotional and spiritual attachments, and supplicants still leave leaf-wrapped fruits tied with bows at the ruins of *heiaus* located in Honolulu's suburbs.

In North America, ancient petroglyphs (figures incised on stone) and pictographs (rock paintings) are found over much of the continent, with especially rich concentrations in Arizona, Utah, Nevada, and New Mexico. Dating techniques are still imprecise, but some Southwest rock art was created thousands of years ago, whereas other pieces may be less than a hundred years old. Several different rock art styles—for example, abstract versus realistic, highly patterned versus relatively free of detail—have been associated with various cultures and time periods; but there seems to be a fundamental continuity in the symbols representing humans, animals, and plants. Certain core concepts (family, kinship, migration, birth, death, and combat) and physical phenomena (clouds, rivers, stars) are represented by symbols that have been consistent over time and place.

Although petroglyphs and pictographs constitute the majority of ancient North American artworks that still remain on their original sites, there are other stoneworks extant. There are the remains, for instance, of medicine wheels—stones forming sacred circles in specially selected natural sites to enhance their spiritual energy. (Some experts also believe they were used to mark the sun's path during the winter and summer solstices.) Medicine wheels can be significant constructions: Wyoming's Big Horn medicine wheel, for instance, has spokes of piled stones measuring 36 feet long radiating out from a central point. These art forms suggest that early Native Americans valued close observation of their natural surroundings as a path to spiritual knowledge and that they celebrated their relationship to the earth through creation of environmental artworks, many of which featured stones.

What significance do today's gardeners find in this legacy of using stone in the landscape for spiritual effects? As the following stone features illustrate, gardeners either adapt the traditions of earlier cultures to their own landscape designs or they carry the spirit, rather than their precise form, into modern pieces.

The Hohokam were a hunting, gathering, and farming society that lived in southern and central Arizona between approximately the first century and 1450. This petroglyph was originally created by Hohokam hunters around 1600 to mark a seasonal camp in the McDowell Mountains, northeast of present-day Phoenix. The images are pecked into a boulder of igneous andesite covered with a reddish brown "desert varnish" of manganese and iron salts. The images, lighter in color because the incision process has removed the varnish, represent human and animal figures. Today the boulder stands in a plaza at Taliesen West, the community Frank Lloyd Wright established in 1932 just outside Scottsdale, Arizona, as a training center for architects. Although federal law prohibits the movement of prehistoric artworks today, it was a common practice in the early decades of this century. With a sensitivity perhaps ahead of its time and place, Wright oriented the newly sited boulder to its original exposure (south-southwest) and used it, as did its original Hohokam creators, to mark a significant spot in the landscape—the entry to his school. As architecture historian Neil Levine notes, the presence of this ancient boulder gives Taliesen West geological and cultural resonances it would otherwise lack. (Taliesen West, Scottsdale, Arizona)

Hawaiians also used large-scale groupings of stones in the landscape, either by collecting and piling them together, as for the walls and platforms of heiaus, or by recognizing the spiritual power already present in naturally sited groups. An example of the latter are the birth stones of Kukaniloko, a picturesque group of thirty-seven boulders located on Oahu's plain of Halemano, a high valley sweeping between the jagged peaks of the island's central mountain ranges. According to tradition, noble wives gave birth lying against these rocks (which were said to be inhabited by guardian spirits able to cut the labor pains) so that their children might gain special honors later in life. Today the Kukaniloko birth stones sit half-buried in the earth under a canopy of palm trees; a fringe of sacred ti shrubs mark them off from surrounding agricultural fields. (Kukaniloko, Oahu, Hawaii)

The Hohokam were a hunting, gathering, and farming society that lived in southern and central Arizona between approximately the first century and 1450. This petroglyph was originally created by Hohokam hunters around 1000 to mark a seasonal camp in the McDowell Mountains, northeast of present-day Phoenix. The images are pecked into a boulder of igneous andesite covered with a reddish brown "desert varnish" of manganese and iron salts. The images, lighter in color because the incision process has removed the varnish, represent human and animal figures. Today the boulder stands in a plaza at Taliesen West, the community Frank Lloyd Wright established in 1932 just outside Scottsdale, Arizona, as a training center for architects. Although federal law prohibits the movement of prehistoric artworks today, it was a common practice in the early decades of this century. With a sensitivity perhaps ahead of its time and place, Wright oriented the newly sited boulder to its original exposure (south-southwest) and used it, as did its original Hohokam creators, to mark a significant spot in the landscape—the entry to his school. As architecture historian Neil Levine notes, the presence of this ancient boulder gives Taliesen West geological and cultural resonances it would otherwise lack. (Taliesen West, Scottsdale, Arizona)

*This is a replica of a shrine that traditionally would be sited
near an ocean beach in Hawaii. The large stone is dedicated to
Kamohoʻalii, the king of sharks, and smaller stones surrounding
it represent a freshwater fish named Oʻope. The upright stones
scattered over the rest of this small site symbolize the eight seas
that folklore says surround the Hawaiian Islands. Another type
of shrine, called a* pohaku ʻaumakua, *or "guardian spirit stone,"
would commonly be located in a family compound to honor the
ancestors. Each stone in such small-scale shrines was gathered
because it exhibited manna (spiritual energy), and grouping a
number of such stones together increased the shrine's spiritual
power exponentially. (Waimea Valley, Oahu, Hawaii)*

The Chinese fascination with stone took many artistic forms. Besides setting prized rocks in gardens, Chinese designers also collected special specimens, mainly dense limestone in shades of black, gray, and later, cream to ash, with fantastically attenuated forms and perforated surfaces, which they called scholars' rocks. These specimens, ranging from 1 inch to 5 feet in height, were placed on wood pedestals in the studies of scholars and government officials, who used them as objects of contemplation meant to remind the viewer of what is natural and, therefore, real. This outdoor sculpture, which evokes associations with both garden stones and scholars' rocks, is surmounted by a dragon—a creature symbolizing power and longevity in Chinese mythology. (Taliesen West, Scottsdale, Arizona)

Hawaiians also used large-scale groupings of stones in the landscape, either by collecting and piling them together, as for the walls and platforms of heiaus, or by recognizing the spiritual power already present in naturally sited groups. An example of the latter are the birth stones of Kukaniloko, a picturesque group of thirty-seven boulders located on Oahu's plain of Halemano, a high valley sweeping between the jagged peaks of the island's central mountain ranges. According to tradition, noble wives gave birth lying against these rocks (which were said to be inhabited by guardian spirits able to cut the labor pains) so that their children might gain special honors later in life. Today the Kukaniloko birth stones sit half-buried in the earth under a canopy of palm trees; a fringe of sacred ti shrubs mark them off from surrounding agricultural fields. (Kukaniloko, Oahu, Hawaii)

Many ancient peoples built their temples on sites they believed possessed special spiritual power. The Maya frequently built theirs over caves, which they considered access points to the underworld. The ceremonial stone steps by which Maya priests and rulers climbed to the tops of their temples were extremely steep, and were designed to make the climber start with right foot forward—a ritual requirement whose meaning is debated today. These granite stone steps leading to a cornfield (by happenstance, corn was a sacred plant to the Maya, as well as their staple of existence) were built in a garden on a Puget Sound island to replicate the steps of an unrestored Maya temple as it might appear in the jungle today, with its individual limestone blocks pushed awry by plants. (Private garden, Bainbridge Island, Washington)

Stonehenge was built in several stages between 3000 and 1800 B.C. by Bronze Age farmers and herders who inhabited Salisbury Plain in south central England. Today most experts agree that the monumental architectural site, which features rings of enormous monoliths and trilothons shaped from sandstone and volcanic rock surrounded by earth embankments, was constructed to mark the movement of the sun and moon as they traverse the sky during the course of a year. Anthony Aveni of Colgate University, who studies the history of ancient astronomy, considers Stonehenge not so much a scientific observatory where a priestly caste observed and calculated complex planetary movements (an interpretation favored by many experts for the last 30 years) but more a sanctuary with a theatrical use, where all members of the community could celebrate special but predictable astronomical events, such as the summer and winter solstices. Whatever its exact use and significance, Stonehenge still casts such a spell on the modern imagination that many replicas and interpretations are scattered throughout the world. This "Stonehenge," made of texturized reinforced concrete, sits in a magnificent setting—a sere bluff standing hundreds of feet above the Columbia River gorge in Washington State. It is on the grounds of a 6,000-acre estate that belonged to railroad magnate Sam Hill, who dedicated it in 1918 as a memorial to local soldiers who died in World War I. (Maryhill Museum, Columbia River gorge, Washington)

The Santa Catalina Mountains northeast of Tucson are part of the Basin and Range Province in southwestern Arizona, a geologically mobile region that for the last 75 million years has experienced repeated collisions and separations associated with shifting tectonic forces. This geology wall was created in Tucson by geologist Doug Shakel with the assistance of stonemason Toby Wright to record the history of the geologic formations that constitute the Santa Catalina range, some of which date to almost two billion years ago.

The wall also happens to be a stunning work of art. Its abstract patterns of color, texture, and shape prove that truth is beauty, and beauty, truth—even when the truth portrayed is simply the history of rocks. There may be no more powerful way to anchor a garden to its natural setting than to enclose it with a geology wall composed of stones native to the area.

The wall presents the formation of the Santa Catalina Mountains from left to right in terms of age and geologic relationships. It begins with Precambrian granites and schists, or basement rocks, dating 1,700–800 million years ago, which are found on the surface only in the northern end of the present-day range. During the late Precambrian age and the Paleozoic era (600–248 million years ago) these mountainous formations slowly eroded and huge inland seas covered the area, depositing numerous layers of sedimentary rocks as they advanced and receded. Later, in the Mesozoic era (248–65 million years ago), igneous activity created the granite and gneiss formations that now form the mass of the Santa Catalinas; but it was only during the Cenozoic era, beginning 65 million years ago, that fault activity uplifted the Santa Catalinas to their present position and height. The detail of wall shown here represents layers of sedimentary rocks, the Apache Group, which settled on top of the basement rock formations between 1,400 and 800 million years ago. (Tohono Chul Park, Tucson, Arizona)

Jens Jensen was the most influential Midwestern landscape designer of his generation; he developed numerous public and private gardens through-out America's heartland during the first decades of the twentieth century. Jensen pioneered the use of native plants and naturalistic landscape designs as part of the wider cultural and artistic movement called the Prairie School, which was developed by Midwestern artists to celebrate the region's unique look and sensibility. He believed, along with earlier master American landscape designers Andrew Jackson Downing and Frederick Law Olmsted, that well-designed public landscapes can promote civic virtue and social cohesion in the larger society. Drawing on his Scandinavian heritage, Jensen often featured stone council rings in his garden designs. The rings, built to emulate the outdoor gathering places where Danes met in democratic assembly as early as the ninth century, served in Jensen's gardens as settings for public performances and meetings. These simple stone rings (usually constructed of a regional limestone) were powerful symbols of participatory democracy, as Jensen hoped it would evolve in American society. (Lincoln Memorial Garden, Springfield, Illinois)

Ten shaman stones covered in forest mosses and liverworts lie in a woodland hollow in a garden on an island in the Pacific Northwest. Driftwood sculptures, adorned with amulets and candles, ring the magic circle. The garden's owner, architect John Braun, gathered these local granitic stones—left as surface debris when glaciers withdrew from northwestern Washington State fifteen thousand years ago—from the surrounding forest and set them here to mark a spot he feels is especially spiritually powerful. Braun considers the stone installation an example of magical art, which he believes possesses the "ability to transform and expand the senses, so they evoke extraordinary responses in the viewer." In this case, the stones represent shamans on the point of entry to a spirit world, where they will encounter transformative experiences leading to knowledge and wisdom. (John C. Braun garden, Whidbey Island, Washington)

This marble statue commemorates the life and death of the garden owners' infant son. The garden is of central importance in their lives, so they chose to site the statue where many of the day's most meaningful activities take place. The statue and the planting bed surrounding it are decorated throughout the year, because the parents want to keep the memory of their child alive through seasonal remembrances. (Sarah Pearl and Barry Sacks garden, Bainbridge Island, Washington)

Useful Stones

Stone, in the form of primitive tools, was one of the earliest materials humans used in an attempt to manipulate their environment. Scientists analyze data on the age, distribution, and design of ancient stone tools (such as scrapers, axes, and projectile points) to chart the beginnings of technology; and they have termed humankind's early history the Old and New Stone Ages, in recognition of the crucial role stone played during this period of our development. Even when iron and bronze eventually supplanted it, stone still retained many practical uses in the landscape. Today's gardeners freely adapt those useful aspects of stone into their garden features, although usually with an eye to stone's decorative or nostalgic qualities.

(Naumkeag, Stockbridge, Massachusetts)

Early peoples all over the world used millstones and grinding stones to prepare grains for cooking; often they incised the millstones' surfaces with attractive grooves and patterns. Japanese gardeners traditionally use old millstones as decorative additions to paths or as freestanding sculptures in a garden vignette. This tropical courtyard features a worn-out millstone, which is almost overrun by bougainvillea escaping from a nearby flowerpot. (Private garden, Honolulu, Hawaii)

Early Native Americans who lived in desert environments developed techniques to divert river water into large canals for their fields of crops: Hundreds of miles of these impressive channels can still be seen scoring the dry landscape surrounding modern Phoenix. But the farmers also used small-scale stone constructions to channel the water that floods the desert floor after rainstorms toward valuable plants. This demonstration plot shows how stones were placed to funnel water toward agaves, plants that were important in the regional economy for food, medicine, and clothing. (Desert Museum, Tucson, Arizona)

Popping up like a decorative mushroom on the lawn of a San Antonio garden, this English straddle stone originally would have been used as one of four identical cornerstones for a medieval granary. The four straddle stones lifted the floor of the granary off the ground to make it inaccessible to rats, who found their inclined trunks and flattened caps impossible to scale. (Pat and Royce Caldwell garden, San Antonio, Texas)

Japanese foresters in the sixteenth through nineteenth centuries lived in charming mountain huts, called minkas, which were made with local materials and simple construction techniques. Because the foresters were forbidden by law to use iron nails, they used stones to weigh down the wooden roof shingles of the huts. Here the roof of a minka reconstructed in Allan Lobb's Washington State garden bears a load of smooth river stones collected from a nearby stream. (Allan Lobb garden, Preston, Washington)

The Japanese gardener's skill in using copper wires to shape the delicate branches of bonsai is an ancient art, but sometimes a full-grown tree requires more drastic measures. Here a large stone weighs down the branch of a Japanese pine (Pinus thunbergiana), *bending it to a more pleasing line over the course of several growing seasons. (Anderson Gardens, Rockford, Illinois)*

Waterworks Park is an 8-acre public site near Seattle, Washington, that acts as the final collection point for storm water that drains from an adjacent 85-acre sewage treatment facility. Designed by environmental artist Lorna Jordan and landscape architect Peggy Gaynor as a series of garden rooms, which together make up the shape of an enormous flower, Waterworks Park features settling and detention ponds, a water funnel, a grotto, and wetlands—all of which function as an integrated system for reclaiming and temporarily storing seasonal runoff. The Grotto, which is the garden room standing at the heart of the design, features walls constructed of shotcrete (a concrete or mortar material pneumatically applied and then sculpted) and flooring made of river rocks and quartzite pavers mortared into intricate designs. Described as a public project that combines "industrial technology, bioengineering, greenway development, and artistic design," the park takes on an increasingly pressing problem in the urban landscape—the need for facilities that can channel and filter excess storm water from impervious surfaces—and uses stone features to create an innovative solution. (Waterworks Park, Renton, Washington)

Eye-Catching Stones

There is a wide variety of readily available stone statues and sculptures—ranging from classical busts to smiling pigs—that can be used to adorn modern American gardens. But some of the most eye-catching artifacts are one-of-a-kind pieces, often made specifically for a particular garden setting. The decorative features illustrated here, some of them dramatic focal points and some merely quiet details, use stone in unusual and clever ways. Their creators have played with the stone's special qualities of color, texture, and shape to make each work memorable.

(Mission San Xavier Del Bac, Arizona)

Smooth, slick river rocks curl into a powerful wave on this California garden wall. The wave's pattern is made from four kinds of river rock, which were gathered near Shasta in northern California and near Salinas in the central coastal area. Stonemason Michael Eckerman mortared them into place onto a concrete block wall that was reinforced with wall ties and bendable metal rods called rebar. (Jonathan Troutner garden, Aptos, California)

An intriguing pattern, copied from a stone wall at Delphi in Greece, winds through this ashlar wall in a Southwest garden. (Santa Fe, New Mexico)

Stones gathered from nearby fields and meadows were dry laid to make this spectacular New England wall. (Great Barrington, Massachusetts)

The pearly sheen and delicate curves of the shells that adorn this poured concrete planter give it an exotic appearance—as though its previous home were in Neptune's seabed garden. Because combining mass-produced items (such as the planter) with found objects (such as marbles, broken pottery, and shells) calls for creativity rather than exceptional skill, it's the kind of project that appeals to weekend artists who want to add handmade, personalized accents to their gardens. Although the shell blooms are at their most decorative in spring, when they reach like candelabras into the branches of a flowering cherry, this imaginative piece has year-round appeal. (Ave Maria Grotto, St. Bernard's Abbey, Cullman, Alabama)

Beginning in the 1930s, Bill Notzke built a rock garden at his Midwestern home using truckloads of stones collected during vacations spent in Arizona, Colorado, and New Mexico. This 12-foot-high moon-and-star arch, made of poured concrete and covered in pink quartz, was Notzke's final piece, built as a memorial to his wife, Ethel, who died in 1963. (Jubilee Rock Gardens, Brimfield, Illinois)

This granitic formation was uncovered by backhoes as they cleared a west Texas field for construction. Set on a natural base in virtually the same spot it was discovered, the stone's fluid lines echo the graceful branches of the native live oaks behind it. (Private garden, Fredericksburg, Texas)

This life-size mountain lion, lean and hungry, crouches atop a 14-foot-high rubble wall in a garden overlooking California's Monterey Bay. Garden owner Paula Adams, who is researching the history of her property, believes Chinese workers, immigrating to California in the 1870s and 1880s to build railroad lines, probably sculpted the big cat at the same time they constructed the exquisitely pieced wall. Both sculpture and wall are made of the granite that underlies most of the Monterey Peninsula; this curious intrusion of igneous rock pierces the western flank of the California coastal ranges, which otherwise consist mainly of folded masses of sedimentary sandstone and chert called Franciscan rock. (The Boulders, Pacific Grove, California)

This piece of mineral calcite from Mexico balances on a sandstone pedestal carved in Bali; it functions as a mobile accent piece that can be set anywhere in the garden where its colors and textures will complement the nearby plants. In late summer, it sits under a Hydrangea serrata *'Preziosa', making an intriguing accompaniment to the shrub's swirled and ruffled maroon-tinged blooms; in spring, the piece is moved near a* Paeonia lutea, *where it provides a deliciously cool contrast to the peony's deep burgundy stems and tender green leaves. (Author's garden, Seattle, Washington)*

An old limestone urn, perched on a wall made of coral blocks, provides habitat for jungle flora in a tropical garden. (Ian M. Ball garden, Coconut Grove, Florida)

The landmass of Hawaii is constantly increasing owing to the large rivers of lava that flow from its active volcanoes. The different kinds of lava cool into shapes and textures so varied that native Hawaiians may have as many terms for lava as the Eskimo peoples have for snow! This lively little lava sculpture peeks out from under strappy tropical foliage in a courtyard garden. (Private garden, Honolulu, Hawaii)

A collection of heart-shaped stones decorates the lawn and planting beds of a Seattle-area garden. (Susan Lombard garden, Redmond, Washington)

visions

Vizcaya The Atmospherics of Stone

The gardens at Vizcaya are a rococo extravaganza of dripping fountains, secret grottoes, sinister mazes, and ornate follies set within the strict borders of formal parterres and allées—all of them moldering away with tropical abandon in the middle of a dark mangrove swamp on the shores of Miami's Biscayne Bay.

Built between 1912 and 1921 for James Deering, heir to the Midwest farm equipment fortune, Vizcaya's house and garden were a joint project of architect F. Burrell Hoffman Jr., landscape designer Diego Suarez, and artist Paul Chalfin. Miami was experiencing rapid growth as a winter playground for America's wealthy classes during this period and Hoffman, Suarez, and Chalfin were well up on contemporary millionaires' taste for mixing European decorative arts from all styles and periods when building their mansions and estate gardens. For Vizcaya's gardens, they used Italian Renaissance and seventeenth-century French motifs—spiced with a dash of pan-European rococo—to create a landscape of dizzying curves, sweeping views, and elaborate ornamentation. Vizcaya's mood is a kind of nerveless degeneracy that floats easily over the grounds' alternating bands of sharp sun and deep shade. The garden, as historian Mac Griswold notes, seems a setting meant for orgies—although orgies of a distinctly melancholy nature.

Stone in its various permutations forms the bedrock of Vizcaya's design. The mansion itself consists of four wings made of steel-reinforced concrete centered on an interior courtyard, but the ten-acre garden's massive walls, stairways, entry gates, and water channels are made of local oolitic limestone, a particularly porous chemical limestone that not only is difficult to carve but also erodes relatively quickly once exposed to Florida's tropical climate.

Vizcaya boasts large numbers of well-preserved sixteenth- and seventeenth-century European marble statues and ornaments, but there also are a considerable array of modern stone artworks made in the same style from the oolitic limestone, and their pitted, abraded, and moss-capped surfaces contribute mightily to the garden's air of noble and ancient decay. Indeed, because most of its garden architecture was carved from blocks of this limestone, which was originally deposited in thick layers under the sea that

Seventeenth-century Italian marble statue. (Vizcaya)

covered the present-day Florida peninsula between 400 and 250 million years ago, it's easy to think of Vizcaya as a gift of the sea—as a kind of alternate-universe Venice that was first built underwater millennia ago, and then suddenly beached on the Florida coast, only slightly eroded, early in the twentieth century.

Vizcaya is a garden of moods created by lines—its restless, disappearing curves alternating with grandly declarative axes arouse feelings of disoriented anticipation in visitors. These lines are virtually all defined by stone, with evergreen plantings in the parterres as a very secondary presence. Because of its sheer size and over-the-top opulence, Vizcaya holds few obvious lessons for the home gardener who contemplates adding a stone feature or two to the back garden, but it remains a compelling place of pilgrimage for those who relish its completely realized vision of stone-driven theatrics.

A walled secret garden features benches carved from marble and native limestone. Vizcaya's architectural features mainly derive from Italian Renaissance hill gardens and classic French gardens of the seventeenth and eighteenth centuries. This giardino segreto is based on the Italian design concept of an enclosed garden area, usually sited adjacent to the living quarters of the house, in which the family can enjoy informal outdoor activities during the afternoon and evening. The secret garden at Vizcaya is located just off the mansion's south and east terraces (which connect to the formal dining room and a tea room); it stands between the dwelling and the mass of the garden, much of which is laid out in the formal parterres and allées characteristic of a classic French garden.

*A maze of stone walls and gates defines the interior spaces of
Vizcaya's gardens. The creamy yellow limestone, with its pocked
and abraded texture, has a softer visual impact than many other
types of stone—it sparkles in the sharp, tropical sunlight, and
even provides a nurturing niche for a wind-borne native plant
(in the upper right-hand corner).*

The semicircular arc of this formal pool is echoed
in the wrought-iron balustrade and the series of
marble columns rising above it. The lion's head
fountains pour their waters down into scalloped
seashells, which overspill into a shallow ledge
rimming the top of the pool; water features that
play on several different levels are also seen in
numerous Italian Renaissance hill gardens. In
most of these Italian gardens, however, the
cascading or dripping water features have been
built into natural hillsides, to take advantage of
gravity's pull. At Vizcaya, this semicircular pool
shares a level surface with a series of elaborate
parterres that spread out before it; therefore, an
artificial vertical drop, consisting of the
balustrade and columns, has been added to
the setting.

Allegorical busts and statues play an important role in classic Italian and French gardens. Drawn from Greek and Roman mythology, these figures can represent aspects of the natural world—Neptune as the seas and oceans, Pomona as the fruits of fields and meadows—or human pursuits that are often identified with the natural world—such as Artemis, goddess of the hunt, pursuing deer with her bow and arrows. Here a bust with classical characteristics that was sculpted by twentieth-century stonemasons stands in a clearing near a mangrove swamp, its head adorned with tropical fruits and its mouth curved in a bibulous grin. It may be modeled a type of statue common in formal Italian, French, and English gardens called

Grottoes played both allegorical and practical roles in classic European gardens. As symbolic entryways to the underworld, they connected earth to otherworldly realms and served as metaphorical bridges between the living and the dead. But they also provided cool resting spots that were especially welcome in hot Mediterranean gardens. The naiad, a type of nymph especially associated with springs and fountains, often decorates the classic European grotto; here she holds up one of the arches that flank a highly patterned niche at Vizcaya.

Coral Castle A Landscape in Magnetic Balance

Although Coral Castle and Vizcaya lie less than thirty miles apart, they inhabit different worlds. A taste for nostalgic fantasy and balmy opulence may have inspired Vizcaya's creators, but more obsessive forces drove Ed Leedskalnin to build the Coral Castle in Homestead, Florida. If Vizcaya's creators drew playfully on a heritage developed by Europe's artists over centuries, Coral Castle served primarily as a testing ground for Leedskalnin's singular philosophical preoccupations with few wider cultural or artistic references. As a result, the Castle stands today as a stark and uncompromising monument to one man's vision of the world and the way it works—a vision that is deeply quirky, but undeniably powerful.

Leedskalnin was a Latvian immigrant who traveled through Canada and the western United States before settling in Florida in 1918. He had trained as a stonemason in his youth; and during his travels, he developed an interest in astronomy and physics. At the age of thirty-one, Leedskalnin

bought an acre of land outside Florida City and began constructing massive sculptures from large blocks of coral quarried on site. Working by himself in secret at night with hand tools that he created from old cars, bicycles, and farm equipment, he sculpted and moved blocks weighing up to 23 tons apiece.

Some of his first, and largest, sculptures represented a crescent moon and the planets Mars and Saturn (opposite page). When Leedskalnin bought a new 10-acre property near Homestead, Florida, in 1936, he moved these 18-foot high monuments by himself under cover of darkness, using a neighbor's tractor. On the new site, Leedskalnin also constructed a 25-foot-high stone telescope, which was permanently trained on the North Star, and an immense sundial, which functioned with some accuracy. Keeping track of the earth's path around the sun was one of his most consistent interests, and many of the monuments at Coral Castle are aligned accordingly.

Crescent moon, Mars, and Saturn. (Coral Castle)

Leedskalnin's works and his secretive building techniques made the Castle increasingly famous in Florida during the late thirties. An intensely private man, Leedskalnin started to build massive walls around the sculptures, some of them from blocks larger than the stones used to construct the Egyptian pyramids and Stonehenge. Because Coral Castle was his home, as well as his playground, Leedskalnin not only built a tower to live in but also the kinds of amenities that any genuine eccentric might want close at hand, such as a fully furnished throne room and a half dozen coral rocking chairs sited to catch the sun's trajectory over the course of the day. Although his home was walled in for privacy, Leedskalnin welcomed visitors, charging them a nominal fee for his personally conducted tours. After Leedskalnin died in 1951, the Coral Castle became a private property that is now permanently open to the public.

The forces that drove Leedskalnin to build Coral Castle are hard to pinpoint. He himself said he built it as a home for a young Latvian girl he referred to only as "Sweet Sixteen," who rejected his offer of marriage but haunted his thoughts for many years. Over time, however, the Castle also became Leedskalnin's laboratory, as he developed numerous idiosyncratic theories about physics and electricity—and most especially, about magnetic currents emanating from the North and South Poles, which he believed were the building blocks of earth's mineral, vegetable, and animal life. Leedskalnin posited that the currents produced individual magnets that, combined with "neutral particles of matter," passed through a chain of beings—stones, vegetation, and humans—in an endless process of dissolution and regeneration. These theories, presented in several pamphlets he wrote in the late 1940s, describe a world of perpetually striving, constantly "pushing and pulling" forces that can achieve balance only when their magnetic currents are aligned correctly.

Is it too fanciful to speculate that Leedskalnin built Coral Castle with such unrelenting determination and backbreaking effort because it represented to him a final bulwark—magnetically balanced and properly aligned—against an otherwise chaotic universe? If so, with what satisfaction he must have closed and barred the Castle's massive stone gate every night, and taken up his position at the telescope, tracking the stars and planets across Florida's deep night sky!

The moon fountain, which Leedskalnin stocked with fish, is composed of three separate pieces, each one representing a phase of the moon as seen from earth. The two curving pieces represent the first and last quarters, and the rounded fountain itself represents the full moon. According to his booklet titled Magnetic Current, *it is only the presence of powerful magnetic streams flowing between the moon and the earth that keep the two from colliding—a delicate balancing act that Leedskalnin monitored with his stone "telescope" almost every night for thirty years.*

ADM. 10¢.

DROP BELOW.

This two-story tower housed a tool and storage room on the first level and Leedskalnin's living quarters on the second level. He lived in quite Spartan circumstances, slinging pieces of burlap between chains hanging from the ceiling to fashion a rough sleeping hammock and a reading chair. Leedskalnin used kerosene for cooking and indoor lighting, and kept food cool by immersing it in a well in glass bottles; a homemade electrical generator supplied power for a radio and for his experiments on magnetism.

Leedskalnin incised a copper panel on the Castle gate with the sun and its path of travel.
He lined up many stone features in the Castle, especially the reclining reading chairs, to take
advantage of the natural light the sun sheds during its daily trajectory.

Tor House
Born of the Rock and the Air

Robinson Jeffers (1887–1962) believed the beauty of the natural world is the ultimate reality and that rocks, stars, the seasons, and natural forces are the signifiers of divine order and meaning. For more than forty years, Jeffers lived on a cliff in Carmel, on California's Monterey Bay, building a house and tower from stones culled from the ocean's beaches and writing poems "that speak [of] the astonishing beauty of things." For Jeffers, both tasks—stonemasonry and writing—ultimately merged, so that in carving out a home for himself in California's coastal landscape he seemed also to be finding his proper place in the universe as a poet and as a human being.

In 1914, shortly after their marriage, Robinson and Una Jeffers came to live in the village of Carmel, which at that time was a small, storm-battered community lying at the end of a long gravel road snaking across the Monterey Bay headlands. Carmel drew them as a refuge from contemporary civilization, among whose evils Jeffers counted overpopulation, war, moral degeneracy, and willful degradation of the natural world. Jeffers argued that an unhealthy human egotism underlay these social and psychological pathologies; he was convinced that humans had to acknowledge their proper (relatively minor) place in the natural world to become spiritually whole. The California Coastal Ranges and Monterey Bay remained his home and spiritual proving ground for the rest of his life.

After twin sons were born to them in 1916, the Jefferses bought land on Carmel Point and engaged a stonemason to build a house of local granitic stone. Over the next several decades, Jeffers became a fine stonemason himself and built walls, terraces, and additions to the house by rolling stones and boulders on ramps from the beach to his property and then positioning them with ropes and pulleys.

Over the years, Jeffers took extended hikes along the California coastline and several trips to New Mexico and Europe; but his essential work—of witnessing and writing about the beauty of the natural world—remained his life's focus. "Jeffers Country," with its crashing seas, rocky beach creeks, wheeling hawks, and fog-hung hills covered in Monterey cypresses, still lives in the reader's imagination as a fully realized evocation of a landscape that embodies the "holy spirit, Beauty."

Tor House, Jeffers's home, was named for several large boulders around which it was built. (*Tor* is an Anglo-Saxon word meaning "stone

Sea-worn granite boulders (Carmel)

outcrop.") Jeffers must have found it metaphysically and aesthetically gratifying to use stone to form the floors and walls of Tor House—his poems mention that his "fingers had the art to make stone love stone" when he made "foundations of sea-worn granite" for the house "born of the rock and the air." Perhaps the most striking edifice at Tor House is Hawk Tower, the four-story stone tower looking out over the ocean; Jeffers built it for his wife. The tower was built of the same beach boulders as the rest of the site's buildings, but it also reflected the Jefferses' fascination with exotic, and potentially spiritually powerful, stone objects. Built into its walls and floors are stones collected from the Great Wall of China, the Irish homes of William Butler Yeats and George Moore, Hawaiian volcanoes, the Michigan farm of Una's family, and other locations around the world either visited by members of the Jeffers family or holding literary or artistic associations for them. Other paths and walls throughout the compound also feature stone objects with farflung associations, all of them helping to make Tor House seem like a small universe built expressly to reflect the interests of the artists living within it.

Jeffers found his inspiration for building Hawk Tower in the tall round towers of medieval Ireland, which were built to warn monasteries and nearby communities of attacks by enemies. They also served as storehouses for books and other treasures and as bell towers for calling the monks to prayer. Hawk Tower and Tor House performed analogous functions for Jeffers, serving as his conning tower, refuge, and source of creativity—all within sight of one of the world's most beautiful stretches of shoreline. Jeffers fit together the stones for his home with the same careful passion that he used in fitting together the words and images of his poems—and both house and poetry endure as memorials to his profound love of the natural world.

Jeffers built Hawk Tower from granite boulders he found on the beach below Tor House. The tower served as a study for Jeffers's wife, Una, who once remarked that she could see "clear across the Pacific" from the tower windows.

as well he longs, fighting else away between house and ocean.

This hillside vignette, dense with the textures, colors, and forms of stone, is as gracefully composed as a Chinese scroll painting of mountain scenery.

Beck incised these graceful portraits of the goddess Kwan Yin and other figures of Chinese mythology on a wall that leads to a brick terrace—the last remnant of the Queen Anne–style mansion that the Becks constructed in 1930, during a period when they were enamoured of the style of the English country house and its garden. Although the Becks continued to live in the house for the rest of their lives, over time they changed their initial design plans for a complementary perennials-and-borders garden into the completely original landscape that constitutes Innisfree today. (The house was demolished, in a dilapidated state, in 1982 at the direction of the Innisfree trustees, who believed its continued, costly maintenance would compromise their mission to preserve the garden. Today visitors can survey the heart of the garden from a knoll where the house originally stood.)

Walker Rock Garden
Agates and Arabesques

Many stone gardeners like to pile rock upon boulder, using sheer size and mass to achieve their desired effect. But Milton Walker was a different kind of artist when it comes to using stone: He delighted in piecing together pebbles, shards of glass, geodes, and semiprecious stones in intricate patterns and mosaics. Walker used them to adorn the walls, terraces, paths, and follies that he constructed in his 10,000-square-foot Seattle garden between 1959 and the early 1980s.

Walker forwent grandeur or overscaled drama and instead worked on an intimate scale, exploiting the colors, shapes, and textures of stones in intricately detailed patterns. The resulting work has an exuberant charm—visitors can still sense the joy with which he must have pored over heaps of agates, crystals, and lava chunks, finding just the right combinations to fill a ready-mortared spot.

Walker was an entirely self-taught artist, but he worked in a tradition with ancient roots. Grottoes decorated with fountains and statues were common in Roman gardens; and by the fifteenth century, European garden designers had resurrected and enhanced the concept by creating grottoes and follies encrusted with shells, coral, pearls, and crystals. The Walker Rock Garden is a variation of these sophisticated garden conceits, one with a colorful folk art twist.

Walker first began using stone in the garden as the result of a mistake; in 1959 he constructed a concrete "lake" on a slope near the back of the house. Disappointed with the way it turned out (he considered the concrete walls too stark), Walker constructed a miniature mountain range around it made from red lava rocks, which he then began to decorate with interesting specimen rocks. After buying ten tons of semiprecious stones from a dealer who was going out of business, Walker started experimenting with making mosaics of birds and butterflies that he used as stepping-stones and wall plaques. Later, Walker began devising more abstract patterns to adorn the freeform arches and tower with which he was filling the garden.

Decorated tower. (Walker Rock Garden)

The last feature that Walker built in his garden was a tower (page 192); it is distinguished from his earlier constructions by having a more fluid line and by demonstrating an especially tight integration between the curves of the structure and the ornamentation that adorns them. As his work matured, it took on some of the fantastical qualities of structures by the Spanish architect Antonio Gaudí; and today the vigorous, curving lines of walls, steps, and arches make satisfyingly complex backdrops to the intricate patterns on their surfaces.

Walker's wife, Florence, says, "He was a generous man, a good man, and I hope visitors can feel some of that good when they visit. And if they get some ideas here to take away to their own gardens, then I think the world will be a little bit better place." As a result of mud slides in the winter of 1997, some of the structures in the lower part of the rock garden need to be stabilized, a task the Walker family hopes local or national arts and garden organizations will undertake to help preserve this unique work of landscape art.

Walker used decorated arches to create complex perspectives and dramatic vistas on a natural slope in his backyard.

walker rock garden

Mosaic stepping-stones set into the lawn lead to the butterfly mural and a decorated terrace nearby.

These butterfly murals are some of the most charming pieces in the Walker Rock Garden. Constructed of cobbles, geodes, and pieces of glass embedded in concrete, their construction marks Walker's transition from creating miniature representational landscapes to more abstract, highly decorative works.

Ohme Gardens
The "Terrible Beauty" of Stone

Every landscape on earth—however placid and peacefully clad in vegetation it may look today—was formed by spectacular geological events and processes. Volcanic eruptions, earthquakes, glaciation, and flooding have left their marks on the mountain ranges, coasts, valleys, plateaus, and deserts that cover the face of the earth. The sequence in which these events took place gives each region its unique topographical profile and shapes the distinctive natural features that make it feel irreplaceably home to the animals and people who inhabit it.

The desolate landscape in eastern Washington State where the rugged, snow-peaked Cascade Mountains collide with the high plains of the Columbia plateau still seems gripped by the raw natural forces that shaped it millions of years ago. Sweeping, miles-long views of undulating mountains, sere valleys, and the stony bluffs that overlook the mighty Columbia River reveal a landscape whose geological scars have not yet been healed by time. This is the dramatic setting in which, in 1929, apple orchardists Herman and Ruth Ohme decided to create a garden.

Ohme Gardens, near Wenatchee, sits near a landscape that was forged by several major cataclysms. Forty to fifty million years ago, a massive subcontinent composed of granite and raised sediments docked high on what was then the northern tier of the west coast of the North American continent. As the subcontinent fused with the older landmass, it created the Cascade Mountains, which today form a spiny ridge traveling in a northeast to southwest direction through the center of Washington State. (Land masses arriving some twenty million years later created the present-day Washington coastline and the beginnings of the Olympic Mountains, now located about one hundred miles to the west of the Cascades.)

Between thirteen and sixteen million years ago, massive flows of molten basalt, some traveling as fast as twenty-five miles an hour, repeatedly flooded the immense high plain, now known as the Columbia Plateau, that covers parts of eastern Washington, eastern Oregon, and western Idaho. The magma flows covered the plateau in layers of basalt that in some areas reached a depth of ten thousand feet.

Twelve to fifteen thousand years ago, a series of enormous floods—some of the largest that have ever occurred on the North American

Wenatchee Valley. (Ohme Gardens)

continent—repeatedly loosed themselves from melting glaciers located in the Rocky Mountains. These floods, which recurred every fifty or sixty years over a period of two thousand years, sent walls of water hundreds of feet high rolling westward from glacial Lake Missoula, in Montana, toward the Pacific. As the floods inundated areas of the Columbia Plateau, they scoured the surface into a terrain of gravelly gorges and coulees that forms the channeled scablands of eastern Washington. Today, the landscape features basalt outcrops, bluffs, and washes covered in a thin, gravelly soil that naturally supports sagebrush and other tough native plants that thrive in arid conditions.

When the Ohmes began creating their garden on a nine-acre rocky bluff overlooking the western edges of the plateau, they took the unusual step of using the desolate natural landscape that surrounded them as their source of inspiration. In 1929, using a model that was neither pretty nor picturesque was a bold and imaginative step for a gardener to take. Originally started as a home garden, it became the major focus of the Ohmes' lives for the next four decades, until a younger generation assumed stewardship of the garden in the early 1970s, by which time it had become a public garden.

In the early years, the Ohmes hauled tons of native basalt, granite, and sedimentary stone up the slopes of the garden in carts pulled by mules. These stones augmented the dramatic natural outcrops already on site and were used to create a series of paths and steps to convey visitors up and down the garden's sometimes dizzying ravines and ridges. In between the outcrops and cliffs, the Ohmes planted flowing alpine meadows that are open to the sky; they also planted thickets of native conifers and shrubs, which today feature forest glades filled with woodland ferns and groundcovers. They planted the sun-drenched outcrops and meadows with a selection of ornamental groundcovers, including large sweeps of *Phlox subulata, Aurinia saxatilis, Vinca minor,* and *Arabis caucasica,* that possess some of the same visual and tactile qualities as alpines and other rock plants: compact foliage, brilliantly colored blooms, and matting or clumping growth habits.

Today, almost seventy years after it was wrested with great imagination and prodigious labor from the desolate landscape around it, Ohme Gardens stands as a quintessential example of mountainous, high-desert terrain, whose most characteristic natural features—stone outcrops, wide sloping meadows, and precipitous ravines—have been isolated, highlighted, and arranged to display their best design possibilities. W. B. Yeats once said that violence sometimes begets a "terrible beauty." He was referring to political violence and its occasionally transfiguring effect on the consciousness of an individual or a nation. The landscape from which Ohme Gardens is carved also possesses a great and unexpected beauty, one that was born in the violence of eruptions, earthquakes, and floods and then transformed by the imaginations of the Ohmes into an artwork that remains true in spirit to its ancient, cataclysmic origins.

Natural basalt outcrops form the bones of Ohme Gardens' design. In the 1920s, the Ohmes recognized the aesthetic potential of these originally desolate crags and spent many subsequent decades releasing their elegant forms from the surrounding landscape.

The Ohmes used tons of local basalt and granite to construct paths and resting spots for the nine-acre garden. The paths rise and fall dramatically as they scale hills and ravines, providing visitors with thrilling views of the countryside for miles in the distance.

The Ohmes chose flowering groundcovers, such as thyme, sedum, pinks, and aubrietas, to hug the hillsides and the fissures between the rocks. Because the Ohmes installed irrigation, they were also free to add moisture-loving plants, such as ferns, as delicate vertical foils to the sprawling groundcovers.

Appendices

Public Gardens with Notable Stone Features

Arizona

Boyce Thompson Southwestern Arboretum
US Route 60
Superior, AZ 85273
520-689-2811

California

Huntington Botanical Garden
1151 Oxford Road
San Marino, CA 91108
818-405-2160

Rancho Santa Ana Botanic Garden
1500 North College Avenue
Claremont, CA 91711-3101
909-625-8767

Strybing Arboretum
Ninth Avenue and Lincoln Way
Golden Gate Park
San Francisco, CA 94122
415-661-1316

University of California Riverside Botanic Gardens
North Campus Circle Drive
Riverside, CA 92521
909-787-4650

Colorado

Betty Ford Alpine Garden
183 Gore Creek Road
Vail, CO 81657
303-476-0103

Denver Botanic Gardens
909 York Street
Denver, CO 80206
303-331-4000

Florida

Fairchild Tropical Gardens
10901 Old Cutler Road
Miami, FL 33156
305-667-1651

Kanapaha Botanical Gardens
4625 Southwest Sixty-third Boulevard
Gainesville, FL 32608
904-372-4981

New Jersey

Leonard J. Buck Garden
RR 2, Layton Road
Far Hills, NJ 07931
201-234-2677

New York

Cornell Plantations
One Plantation Road
Ithaca, NY 14850
607-255-3020

New York Botanical Garden
200th Street and Kazimiroff Boulevard
Bronx, NY 10458-5126
718-817-8700

Ohio

Cox Arboretum
6733 Springboro Pike
Dayton, OH 45449
513-434-9005

Oregon

Berry Botanic Garden
11505 Southwest Summerville Avenue
Portland, OR 97219
503-636-4112

Washington

Bellevue Botanical Garden
12001 Main Street
Bellevue, WA 98008
425-451-3755

Rhododendron Species Botanical Garden
Weyerhauser Corporate Headquarters
Federal Way, WA 98063-3798
253-661-9377

Wisconsin

Olbrich Botanical Garden
3330 Atwood Avenue
Madison, WI 53704
608-246-4551

Asian Gardens

Alabama

Birmingham Botanical Gardens—Japanese Garden
2612 Lane Park Road
Birmingham, AL 35223
205-879-1227

California

Hakone Gardens
21000 Big Basin Way
Saratoga, CA 95070
408-741-4994

Huntington Botanical Gardens—Japanese Garden
1151 Oxford Road
San Marino, CA 91108
818-405-2141

Florida

Society of Four Arts—Chinese Courtyard
Royal Palm Way
Palm Beach, FL 33480
561-655-7226

Hawaii

Byodo-In Temple
47-200 Kahekili Highway
Kaneohe, HI 96744

Illinois

Anderson Gardens
2214 Stoneridge Drive
Rockford, IL 61107
815-877-2525

Chicago Botanic Garden—Japanese Garden
775 Dundee Road
Glencoe, IL 60022
847-835-5440

Missouri

Missouri Botanical Garden—Japanese Garden
2315 Tower Grove Avenue
Saint Louis, MO 63110
314-577-5100

New York

Brooklyn Botanic Garden—Japanese Garden
1000 Washington Avenue
Brooklyn, NY 11225
718-622-4433

Innisfree Garden
RR 2, Tyrrel Road
Millbrook, NY 12545
914-677-8000

John P. Humes Japanese Stroll Garden
Dogwood Lane
Mill Neck, NY 11765
516-676-4486

Oregon

Portland Japanese Garden
611 Kingston Avenue SW
Portland, OR 97208
503-223-4070

Pennsylvania

Swiss Pines, The Arnold Bartschi Foundation
Charlston Road
Malvern, PA 19355
215-933-6916

Texas

Fort Worth Botanic Garden—Japanese Garden
3220 Botanic Garden Drive
Fort Worth, TX 76107
817-871-7685

Washington

Bloedel Reserve
7571 Northeast Dolphin Way
Bainbridge Island, WA 98110-1097
360-842-7631

Kubota Gardens
Renton Avenue S and Fifty-fifth Avenue S
Seattle, WA 98111
206-684-4584

Washington Park Arboretum—Japanese Garden
2300 Arboretum Drive E
Seattle, WA 98112
206-543-8800

Display Gardens, Sites, Parks, and Grounds

Alabama

Ave Maria Grotto
Saint Bernard's Abbey
1600 St. Bernard Drive SE
Cullman, AL 35056
205-734-4110

Arizona

Arizona-Sonora Desert Museum
2021 North Kinney Road
Tucson, AZ 85743
520-883-2702

Mystery Castle
800 East Mineral Street
Phoenix, AZ 85047
602-268-1581

Tohono Chul Park
7366 North Paseo Del Norte
Tucson, AZ 85704
520-575-8468

California

Lummis Home State Historic Monument
200 East Avenue 43
Los Angeles, CA 90031
213-222-0546

Tor House
Robinson Jeffers Tor House Foundation
P.O. Box 2713
Carmel, CA 93921
408-624-1813

Florida

Coral Castle
28655 South Dixie Highway
Homestead, FL 33033
305-248-6344

Society of the Four Arts
Royal Palm Way
Palm Beach, FL 33176
561-655-7226

Vizcaya
3251 South Miami Boulevard
Miami, FL 33129
305-250-9133

Georgia

Swan House
Atlanta History Center
3101 Andrews Drive
Atlanta, GA 30305
404-814-4082

Louisiana

Hodges Gardens
US Route 71
Many, LA 71449
318-586-3523

Massachusetts

Naumkeag
P.O. Box 792
Stockbridge, MA 01262
413-298-3239

New Jersey

Devereux Deerhaven
230 Pottersville Road
Chester, NJ 07930
908-879-4500

New York

Innisfree Garden
RR 2, Tyrrel Road
Millbrook, NY 12545
914-677-8000

Manitoga
P.O. Box 249
Garrison, NY 13827
914-424-3812

Sonnenberg Gardens
151 Charlotte Street
Canandaigua, NY 14424
716-394-4922

Oregon

Petersen's Rock Gardens
7 miles south of US Highway 97
Redmond, OR 97756
541-382-5574

Texas

Brackenridge Park Oriental Garden
3903 North Saint Mary's Street
San Antonio, TX 78212
210-321-3000

National Wildflower Research Center
4801 La Crosse Avenue
Austin, TX 78739
512-292-4200

Virginia

Maymont
1700 Hampton Street
Richmond, VA 23220
804-358-7166

Washington

The Chase Garden (in Orting WA)
P.O. Box 98553
Des Moines, WA 98198

Maryhill Museum of Art—Stonehenge
35 Maryhill Museum Drive
Goldendale, WA 98620
509-773-3733

Ohme Gardens
3327 Ohme Road
Wenatchee, WA 99353
509-662-5785

Walker Rock Garden
Seattle, WA
206-935-3036

Washington, DC

Dumbarton Oaks
1703 Thirty-second Street
Washington, DC 20007
202-342-3200

Glossary

adobe a sun-dried mixture of clay and straw, used as a building material primarily in the southwestern United States. It is either shaped into bricks or used as a surface covering for walls made of stone or rubble.

agate a type of mineral quartz featuring indistinguishably small crystals in a wide variety of colors, banding patterns, and translucencies. Often found in cavities in volcanic rocks.

alpine meadow a meadow in mountainous terrain that is located above the tree line and below the permanent snow line.

andesite an extrusive igneous rock containing iron and magnesium; found in the Cascade Mountains of Washington State and the McDowell Mountains outside Phoenix, Arizona.

arroyo in arid landscapes, a steep gully that acts as a temporary channel for runoff water during flash floods.

ashlar any kind of stone that is cut and shaped for use in construction.

axis a central reference line around which a formal garden plan is organized.

ballast stone or other heavy materials placed in the hold of a ship to promote stability.

basalt a fine-grained igneous rock that is strong and weather resistant; in gardens it is usually used for walls, stepping-stones, pavers, and specimen pieces.

basement rock igneous and metamorphic rock that underlies sedimentary deposits; usually Precambrian in origin.

bedrock the solid rock that lies under soil, gravel, or unconsolidated sediments.

bluestone a sandstone with blue-gray coloring that is commonly shaped into flagstones for use in garden construction.

caliche a Southwest desert construction material composed of gravel, sand, and calcium carbonate; used in a manner similar to adobe.

chert another term for flint, a tough rock that often appears in nodules that accumulate on limestone; can be shaped into sharp-edged tools and weapons.

cirque a half-circle hollowed from the side of a mountain by the movement of glaciers.

columnar joints long, many-sided columns formed in basalt during the process of cooling and contraction.

coral underwater formations composed of the calcified skeletons of marine animals; sometimes carved into blocks and used as a building material.

cordillera parallel mountain ranges and the formations, such as valleys and plains, lying between them.

coulee a long gorge originally formed by erosion caused by flooding; a characteristic formation in the channeled scablands of eastern Washington State.

desert varnish a warm reddish brown patina formed by iron salts on the surface of stones in desert areas.

dry stone construction stacking stones in walls without the use of mortar or concrete.

erratics boulders of exotic origin that have been deposited in a landscape by the action of glaciers; sometimes called haystack rocks.

extrusive rock igneous rock that erupts onto the surface of the earth as a result of volcanic activity and lava flows.

fault a fracture in the surface of the earth.

fissure a vertical crack in a rock formation.

flagstone any kind of stone shaped into flat pavers for use in garden construction.

fluvial plain a level area of land through which a river flows.

geode a hollow in a small rock formation that is filled with crystal formations surrounded by banded minerals.

geological periods the major divisions of geologic time, including the Precambrian (before 570 million years ago), the Paleozoic (570–230 million years ago); the Mesozoic (230–65 million years ago); and the Cenozoic (beginning 65 million years ago).

glaciation the shaping of a landscape by the movement of advancing or retreating glaciers.

gneiss a coarse-grained metamorphic stone that is strong and weather resistant; in gardens it is usually used in rockeries or as a specimen piece.

granite an igneous rock that is strong and dense; in gardens it is used in walls, pavers, stepping-stones, and as specimen pieces.

hypertufa a mixture of sand, concrete, and peat moss that is combined with water and molded to create planters that resemble sandstone troughs in color and texture. Some gardeners substitute perlite or vermiculite for the sand.

ice age a period of extensive glacial activity, with consequent effects on geology and plant and animal life.

ice cap a mass of ice covering an area approximately smaller in size than twenty thousand square miles; an ice sheet covers larger areas—the Laurentide ice sheet, for instance, covered major parts of present-day eastern Canada and New England until its retreat northward, which occurred around 15,000 B.C.

jade refers to two separate minerals—nephrite (found in New Zealand and Canada) and jadeite (found in South and Central America and China)—that share similar qualities, including extreme hardness and colors ranging from emerald through brown, cream, and yellow. Jade is considered a magical object by many ancient peoples, and has been used for jewelry and tools since prehistory.

karst land formed over layered deposits of limestone and dolomite; the topography is frequently pitted by collapsed sinkholes and caves that, owing to chemical weathering, form wherever the rock formations become sufficiently brittle to collapse.

lava molten rock that erupts or flows from a volcano; in its cooled state, lava is easily shaped or carved for use in garden construction.

ledge a shelf or step protruding from a rock outcrop.

limestone a sedimentary rock often used as cut stone in garden construction because it tends to split easily; a preferred stone for construction of rock gardens.

magma molten rock or rock particles lying underneath the earth's crust that may erupt to the earth's surface.

mantle the layer of the earth, consisting of molten rock, that lies above the core and below the crust

mesa a mountain whose top has been leveled by massive floods or erosion, usually with one or more steep cliff sides.

mortar a mixture of cement and aggregates, such as sand, lime, and fireclay, that is used in stonemasonry.

oolite a limestone composed of ooliths, which are small accretions formed of calcium carbonate and sand.

orogeny the process by which mountains are formed.

outcrop bare rock formations protruding from the earth's surface.

petroglyph a design pecked or carved into rock and stone.

pictograph a design painted on rock and stone.

plate tectonics a generally accepted geological theory which asserts that the earth is covered by rigid plates that fuse, overlap, and tear away from each other, forming oceans and continents in the process.

plutonic rock rock formed deep below the earth's crust by heat and pressure; usually granitic in composition.

pudding stone a conglomerate of small pebbles and cementing stone particles.

rhyolite an igneous rock with a composition similar to granites that has attractive "banding" patterns on its surface; often used as a specimen stone in gardens.

rock types igneous, metamorphic, and sedimentary. Igneous rock is formed of solidified magma; metamorphic rocks are igneous, sedimentary, or other types of metamorphic rocks whose structure and composition are altered by intense heat and/or pressure; sedimentary rock is composed of the consolidated debris of igneous, metamorphic, or other sedimentary rocks deposited in layers.

rubble uncut stone used in garden construction.

sandstone a sedimentary rock, composed mostly of quartz particles, that splits easily for use in garden construction.

scabland a high desert area overlaying basalt flows; dry channels carved into such topography by massive floods.

schist metamorphic rock with a flaky surface that erodes easily; especially valued by Japanese gardeners as a specimen stone.

scree an accumulation of angular rock fragments found at the base of a cliff or steep slope.

slate a mudstone that metamorphosed into flat, multilayered, erosion-resistant sheets.

spit a narrow point of soil, sand, or gravel extending into a body of water.

swale a marshy depression in a tract of land.

tabby a building material, mainly used in the Southeast, composed of crushed oyster shells and lime.

t'ai hu rock limestone specimen stones especially prized by Chinese gardeners for their complex shapes and textures.

talus large-scale rock debris found at the base of cliffs or slopes.

till a mixture of clay, sand, silt, and gravel deposited by glacial action.

tor an Anglo-Saxon word meaning a stone outcrop.

trilithon a stone structure consisting of two parallel, vertical supports with a horizontal capstone bridging them at the top: Stonehenge's five trilithons may be the most famous examples still extant.

tufa a sedimentary stone composed of calcium carbonate; used for carved stone troughs because it is porous and easily worked.

wash a dry, gravelly bed in the floor of a canyon.

wetlands a tract of land whose soils are saturated with water for significant portions of the year; often a haven for native plants and wildlife as well as a seasonal storage area and filtration point for runoff surface waters.

Selected Readings

Garden Styles

Adams, William Howard. *Grounds for Change: Major Gardens of the Twentieth Century.* Boston: Little, Brown, 1993.

Chatfield, Judith. *The Classic Italian Garden.* New York: Rizzoli, 1991.

Davidson, A. K. *The Art of Zen Gardening.* Los Angeles: Tarcher, 1983

Eaton, Leonard K. *Landscape Artist in America: the Life and Works of Jens Jensen.* Chicago: University of Chicago Press, 1964.

Engel, David H. *Creating a Chinese Garden.* Portland, Oreg.: Timber Press, 1986.

Ji, Cheng. *The Craft of Gardens.* Translated by Alison Hardie. New Haven, Conn.: Yale University Press, 1988.

Karson, Robin S. *Fletcher Steele, Landscape Architect: An Account of a Gardenmaker's Life, 1885–1971.* New York: Abrams, 1989.

Keswick, Maggie. *The Chinese Garden: History, Art & Architecture.* New York: St. Martin's Press, 1986.

Masson, Georgina. *Italian Gardens.* New York: Abrams, n.d.

McGuire, Diane Kostial. *American Garden Design: An Anthology of Ideas That Shaped Our Landscape.* New York: Macmillan, 1994.

Miller, Naomi. *Heavenly Caves: Reflections on the Garden Grotto.* New York: Brazillier, 1982.

Mitford, Mary Russell. *My Garden: A Nineteenth-Century Writer on Her English Cottage Garden.* Boston: Houghton Mifflin, 1990.

Morris, Edwin T. *The Gardens of China: History, Art, and Meanings.* New York: Scribner's, 1983.

O'Gorman, James F. *Three American Architects: Richardson, Sullivan, and Wright, 1865–1915.* Chicago: University of Chicago Press, 1991.

Plumptre, George. *The Garden Makers: The Great Tradition of Garden Design from 1600 to the Present Day.* New York: Random House, 1993.

Scott-James, Anne. *The Cottage Garden.* New York: Penguin, 1982.

Slawson, David A. *Secret Teachings in the Art of Japanese Gardens.* Tokyo: Kodansha, 1987.

Yaeger, Bert D. *The Hudson River School: American Landscape Artists.* New York: Smithmark, 1996.

Habitats

Foster, H. Lincoln. *Rock Gardening.* Portland, Oreg.: Timber Press, 1982.

Halpin, Anne. *Rock Gardens.* New York: Potter, 1997.

Kruckeberg, Arthur R. *Gardening with Native Plants of the Pacific Northwest.* Seattle: University of Washington Press, 1989.

Lawrence, Elizabeth. *A Rock Garden in the South.* Durham, N.C.: Duke University Press, 1990.

Schafer, Jean-Paul, and John Rodgers, eds. *The Anatomy of Mountain Ranges.* Princeton, N.J.: Princeton University Press, 1987.

Thomas, Graham Stuart. *The Rock Garden and Its Plants: From Grotto to Alpine House.* Portland, Oreg.: Timber Press, 1989.

Wasowski, Sally, and Andy Wasowski. *Native Gardens for Dry Climates.* New York: Potter, 1995.

Young, Louise B. *The Blue Planet: A Celebration of the Earth.* Boston: Little, Brown, 1983.

Stone Art

Aveni, Anthony. *Stairway to the Stars: Skywatching in Three Great Ancient Cultures.* New York: Wiley, 1997.

Chauvet, Jean-Marie. *Dawn of Art: the Chauvet Cave, the Oldest Known Paintings in the World.* New York: Abrams, 1996.

Chronic, Halka. *Pages of Stone: Geology of Western National Parks & Monuments.* Seattle: Mountaineers, 1986.

Cox, J. Halley. *Hawaiian Petroglyphs.* Honolulu: Bishop Museum Press, 1970.

Mowry, Robert D. *Worlds Within Worlds: The Richard Rosenblum Collection of Chinese Scholar's Rocks.* Cambridge, Mass.: Harvard University Art Museums, 1996.

Sabloff, Jeremy. *The New Archaeology and the Ancient Maya.* New York: Scientific American Press, 1990.

Townsend, Robert, ed. *The Ancient Americas: Art from Sacred Landscapes.* Chicago: The Art Institute of Chicago, 1992.

Visions

Allen, John Eliot, and Marjorie Burns. *Cataclysms on the Columbia.* Portland, Oreg.: Timber Press, 1986.

Cloud, Preston. *Oasis in Space: Earth History from the Beginning.* New York: Norton, 1986.

Collins, Lester. *Innisfree: An American Garden.* New York: Abrams, 1994.

Griswold, Mac, and Eleanor Weller. *The Golden Age of American Gardens: Proud Owners, Private Estates, 1890–1940.* New York: Abrams, 1991.

Woodford, A. O. *Historical Geology.* San Francisco: Freeman, 1965.

Index